low-carb cooking

low-carb cooking

LOSE WEIGHT AND IMPROVE YOUR HEALTH THE EASY WAY WITH THIS CLEVERLY BALANCED DIET

ANNE CHARLISH

LORENZ BOOKS

This edition is published by Lorenz Books

Lorenz Books is an imprint of Anness Publishing Ltd
Hermes House, 88–89 Blackfriars Road, London SE1 8HA
tel. 020 7401 2077; fax 020 7633 9499; www.lorenzbooks.com; info@anness.com

UK agent: The Manning Partnership Ltd, 6 The Old Dairy, Melcombe Road, Bath BA2 3LR
tel. 01225 478444; fax 01225 478440; sales@manning-partnership.co.uk

UK distributor: Grantham Book Services Ltd, Isaac Newton Way, Alma Park Industrial Estate, Grantham, Lincs NG31 9SD
tel. 01476 541080; fax 01476 541061; orders@gbs.tbs-ltd.co.uk

North American agent/distributor: National Book Network, 4501 Forbes Boulevard, Suite 200, Lanham, MD 20706
tel. 301 459 3366; fax 301 429 5746; www.nbnbooks.com

Australian agent/distributor: Pan Macmillan Australia, Level 18, St Martins Tower, 31 Market St, Sydney, NSW 2000
tel. 1300 135 113; fax 1300 135 103; customer.service@macmillan.com.au

New Zealand agent/distributor: David Bateman Ltd, 30 Tarndale Grove, Off Bush Road, Albany, Auckland
tel. (09) 415 7664; fax (09) 415 8892

Publisher: Joanna Lorenz
Managing Editor: Linda Fraser
Senior Editor: Susannah Blake
Copy Editor: Rosie Hankin
Editorial Reader: Joy Wotton
Recipes: Alex Barker, Joanna Farrow, Brian Glover, Nicola Graimes, Sallie Morris and Kate Whiteman
Designer: Blue Banana
Photographers: Nicki Dowey (introduction) and Tim Auty, Gus Filgate,
Amanda Heywood, William Lingwood and Thomas Odulate (recipes)
Home Economists: Beth Heald (introduction) and Joanna Farrow, Kate Jay, Lucy McKelvie,
Joy Skipper and Sunil Vijayakar (recipes)

Previously published as *Low Carbohydrate Diet for Health*

10 9 8 7 6 5 4 3 2 1

NOTES
Bracketed terms are intended for American readers.

For all recipes, quantities are given in both metric and imperial measures and, where appropriate, measures are also given in
standard cups and spoons. Follow one set, but not a mixture, because they are not interchangeable.

Standard spoon and cup measures are level. 1 tsp = 5ml, 1 tbsp = 15ml, 1 cup = 250ml/8fl oz

Australian standard tablespoons are 20ml. Australian readers should use 3 tsp in place of 1 tbsp for measuring small
quantities of gelatine, flour, salt, etc.

Medium (US large) eggs are used unless otherwise stated.

The diets and information in this book are not intended to replace advice from a qualified practitioner, doctor or dietician.
Always consult your health practitioner before adopting any of the suggestions in this book. Neither the author nor the
publishers can accept any liability for failure to follow this advice.

contents

introduction

eating for health

A HEALTHY DIET SHOULD PROVIDE you with all the essential nutrients necessary to maintain good health. These include carbohydrates, proteins, fats, vitamins, minerals and water. The body needs fuel in the form of food to generate the energy that we need to keep us warm and to carry out our everyday activities, both physical and mental.

THE LOW-CARBOHYDRATE DIET

Chief among the constituents of the foods we consume are carbohydrates, proteins and fats. The low-carbohydrate diet is low in carbohydrates and relatively high in proteins and fats. The thinking behind this diet is that some carbohydrates, although not all types, cause our bodies to create and store fat, which will ultimately lead to unhealthy weight gain.

Carbohydrates can be defined as all starches and sugars, including all grains, cereals, potatoes and the foods that are made from them. On a low-carbohydrate diet, these foods should form only a very limited part of the daily diet. You may, however, eat as much meat, poultry, fish and shellfish as you like, as well as some fats, oils and dairy products (including cream, butter, yogurt and cheese), most green vegetables and some fruits. You can eat all of these foods until you no longer feel hungry and, best of all, you need not count calories. It is also very important to drink plenty of water when following a low-carbohydrate diet.

BURNING FAT

The low-fat/high-carbohydrate diet that is favoured by many today starves the body of calories, proteins and fat. This causes the body to burn large amounts of body fat and muscle in order to provide itself with fuel. When following this type of diet, you will lose weight, but the loss of muscle tissue not only shows up physically, making you look flabby and untoned, but it also reduces the body's metabolic rate. This means that if you wish to continue losing weight in the long term, you will need to cut your calorie intake still further.

In contrast, on a low-carbohydrate diet the body burns mostly fat and preserves lean muscle tissue. If you do any exercise — something that is always recommended on any diet — you will add lean muscle while still losing fat. Exercise will also increase your metabolic rate and thus help to increase the loss of fat.

CARBOHYDRATES AND BLOOD SUGAR

When carbohydrates are consumed, the body changes them into the sugars glucose and glycogen that fuel muscles, the nervous system and the brain. Foods that are high in carbohydrate cause our blood sugar levels to rise and, in reaction to this, the pancreas secretes the hormone insulin to help lower these levels by storing the sugar elsewhere. A limited amount of glycogen stored in the liver and muscle tissue, while any remaining sugars are stored as body

Left: *On a low-carbohydrate diet, you should eat high-protein, low-carbohydrate foods such as fish, shellfish, lean meat and cottage cheese. You should also drink at least eight glasses of water a day.*

"Bad" carbohydrates such as sweet snacks, cakes and cookies made from refined white sugar and flour can cause a huge rise in blood sugar levels and a consequent secretion of insulin. Blood sugar levels will then drop sharply as the sugars in the blood are stored as fat and you can be left feeling both hungry and irritable.

The entry rate of a carbohydrate into the bloodstream is known as its glycaemic index (GI). The lower the glycaemic index, the slower the rate of absorption. The glycaemic index is determined by the structure of the simple sugars in the food, the soluble fibre content and the fat content. The glycaemic index ranks foods on how they affect our blood sugar levels, and measures how much your blood sugar increases in the two or three hours after eating. Several hundred foods have now been assessed for their glycaemic quality. Pure glucose has a GI rating of 100 and is rapidly absorbed into the bloodstream.

The ideal is to eat foods that maintain a fairly consistent blood sugar level, and this is what protein and fats do. Carbohydrates can produce peaks and troughs of energy. A low-carbohydrate diet will help you to maintain more stable blood sugar levels by restricting your intake of carbohydrates with high GI. Consuming only proteins, fats and carbohydrates with a low GI, such as salad leaves, vegetables and wholegrains, will help you to avoid fluctuating blood sugar levels.

AVOIDING FLUCTUATING BLOOD SUGAR LEVELS

When you are hungry, it is often tempting to seize the first snack that comes to hand for instant sustenance. To avoid unhealthy snacking, go through the refrigerator and store cupboard and replace sweet, starchy foods with a supply of healthy, nutritious, low-carbohydrate foods such as tuna fish, mackerel, sardines, canned tomatoes and fresh vegetables. If hunger strikes, reach for one of these low-carbohydrate foods that will provide sustained energy and avoid the sudden "sugar-rush" and subsequent drop in energy provided by sugary, starchy snacks.

HOW YOU SHAPE UP

The first thing you should ascertain before you embark on a low-carbohydrate diet is whether or not you need to lose weight. One of the measures routinely used to assess healthy weight is the BMI (Body Mass Index). This is considered to be the most valid measure of weight status, and is far more reliable than using weight tables.

To calculate your BMI:
1 Weigh yourself, undressed, in kilograms. (If you weigh yourself in pounds, divide this number by 2. 2.)
2 Measure your height in metres, then multiply it by itself. (If you take your height in inches, divide it by 39. 4, then multiply the result by itself.)
3 Divide the result of 1 by the result of 2. This is your Body Mass Index.

For example, if your weight is 65kg and your height 1.68 metres, you will have a BMI of 23: 65 ÷ (1. 68 x 1. 68) = 23

Most health experts and nutritionists agree that people with a BMI of between 20 and 25 – the optimum measure – have a lower risk of illnesses such as heart disease, high blood pressure and stroke; those with a BMI of 25 to 30 have a moderate risk (though need not be too concerned); and those with a BMI of over 30 are at a proportionately greater risk. The over-30 group is also more likely to contract diseases, such as arthritis, affecting the joints and muscles, and a BMI of over 40 poses a serious health risk. You should not aim to reduce your BMI below 20.

evolving attitudes towards carbohydrates

AS THE HUMAN RACE HAS EVOLVED, so too has their diet. In primitive times, people ate a diet rich in simple, unrefined carbohydrates in the form of plant materials, and proteins and fats obtained from the animals they hunted. The enormous changes that have occured to human lifestyle and diet since then have led to the need to reassess what we should eat.

In early times, people led active, physical lifestyles, hunting animals and gathering foods from the land. As people began to grow their own food, grains and dairy products were introduced into the diet and then, with the industrialization and mechanization that has occurred over the last few hundred years, the human diet and lifestyle has changed radically.

As people and societies developed, it was often seen as a sign of wealth to be able to afford fish and meat and only the very poor had to survive on vegetables, and staples such as potatoes and bread.

In the second half of the 20th century, the increasing affluence that followed the Second World War meant that people could jettison the old wartime ideas of growing their own vegetables and baking their own bread, and feast on a more opulent diet. The high protein diet came into vogue and few people could see the benefits of eating complex carbohydrates.

With the increasing mechanization of society, people were leading more and more sedentary lifestyles and eating more refined foods. Fewer people were walking to their workplace and mass forms of travel,

together with the arrival of the car at prices that many could afford, meant that people were storing fat from their diet rather than using it for energy as they had in the past.

By the 1970s, it was recognized that people were eating far too many simple carbohydrates and too much protein and animal fat for optimum health, and that efficient digestion relied on the intake of complex carbohydrate and fibre. People were advised to eat wholemeal (wholewheat) bread and wholemeal pasta and at least five servings of fruit and vegetables a day, and to cut down on protein and fats.

Today, research practice has come full circle and it has been acknowledged that no one can live exclusively on fibre. People need to include protein and fats in their diet, some people need less carbohydrate than others, and some people may even become addicted to carbohydrate and the energy that it brings. Most people no longer need the large amounts of energy that were needed in the past – unless they lead a very physical, active lifestyle.

Nowadays, many health professionals are advising people to cut down on their high intake of carbohydrates, particularly refined carbohydrates, while at the same time, acknowledging that carbohydrates still play a key role in any healthy diet.

Left: *Meals that are rich in carbohydrate and low in protein and fat, such as large servings of white pasta with a sauce, may not be as healthy as once thought. Many health professionals are advising people to cut down on their intake of these foods.*

CARBOHYDRATES THAT ARE NEEDED FOR GOOD HEALTH

Carbohydrates are the body's chief source of energy. Complex carbohydrates can be found in the starch of foods of plant origin, such as wheat and cereals, beans, potatoes and all fruit and vegetables. The body changes these carbohydrates into glucose and glycogen to fuel muscles, the nervous system and the brain. Because of this, in the last 20 years, much of the emphasis on good nutrition has focused on the need for carbohydrate. This emphasis on eating carbohydrates has also partly been a reaction against the fashion for high-protein diets that was prevalent in the preceding years.

The healthiest sources of carbohydrates are wholegrains, which can be found in wholemeal (whole-wheat) bread and flour, beans and lentils, wholemeal pastas and brown rice. The calories obtained from these carbohydrates burn the fastest of all

Below: Complex carbohydrates, found in wholemeal (whole-wheat) grains, pasta and beans, provide slow-release energy that is less easily converted into body fat.

and are not so easily converted into body fat. They are particularly useful for toning up the digestive processes of the body. We can also find good carbohydrate in the natural sugars (fructose) of most fruit and some vegetables.

The most important point about unrefined carbohydrates is their slow conversion into sugars in the body. These foods are released into the bloodstream gradually and therefore provide a source of long-term energy. For this reason, complex carbohydrates are particularly useful in sports and fitness training. For athletes and professional sports players, the banana is the ultimate carbohydrate energy booster.

The problem with carbohydrate intake comes only with refined carbohydrates in the form of refined white sugar and flour products from which most or all of the health-giving nutrients have been removed during processing. These foods are quickly absorbed into the bloodstream leading to a sudden and rapid rise in blood sugar levels. In a bid to reduce these levels as quickly as possible, the pancreas releases insulin, which allows the body to store the excess sugars as body fat. The instant burst

Above: Fruit contains the natural sugar fructose, which is much kinder to the body than refined white sugar.

of energy that is felt after consuming these carbohydrates is soon followed by fatigue and renewed hunger as the sugars are removed from the blood and stored. In some people, a variety of health problems and disorders may arise from the constant rise and fall of blood sugar levels.

Above: Simple carbohydrates such as white sugar and pasta and bread made from refined flour are quickly absorbed and lead to a rapid rise in blood sugars.

carbohydrates that damage your health

In light of current research, the high-carbohydrate diet, which has been so popular for many years, is increasingly being called into question. Many believe that a diet consisting mainly of simple carbohydrates cannot cannot supply the body with th building blocks that are essential for good health and can, in fact, cause many health problems from hormonal imbalance and diabetes to weight gain and heart disease.

Nutritionists are coming to believe that a diet made up of carbohydrate, with very little fat and protein, cannot supply the body with sufficient vitamins and minerals. They maintain that because carbohydrate stimulates the digestive system, any nutrients that are present will pass through the body too quickly to be of value. More worryingly, it is also thought that a diet high in simple carbohydrates may disrupt a number of the body's usual mechanisms. These include:

- hormonal imbalances
- hyperinsulinism
- chronic weight gain
- diabetes
- high blood fat levels, which may lead to atherosclerosis and heart disease, or exacerbate those conditions if they already exist
- disorders of the digestive system, including irritable bowel syndrome
- chronic fatigue
- carbohydrate addiction

HORMONAL IMBALANCES

It is thought that, in some people, too much carbohydrate, particularly the wrong types of carbohydrates, can adversely affect the functioning of the endocrine system. The endocrine system consists of glands (such as the thyroid gland and the pituitary gland) that secrete hormones into the bloodstream.

Right: *Many health problems can be attributed to over consumption of the wrong types of carbohydrate.*

These hormones then stimulate particular cells or tissues into a specific action, maintaining balance and health within the body – for example, the pancreas secretes the hormone insulin to maintain stable blood sugar levels. An underactive thyroid gland can cause obesity that no amount of dieting will ever be able to resolve. Swings in blood sugar levels are known to occur in response to the consumption of "bad" carbohydrates, and this can be even more pronounced in women in the days preceding menstruation when they may experience carbohydrate cravings.

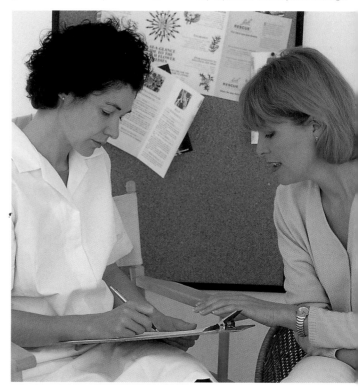

ght: *A traditional breakfast of quickly
sorbed carbohydrates such as fruit, toast
d fruit juice is not appropriate on a low-
rbohydrate diet. It will provide a rush
sugars, followed by a release of insulin
d a sharp drop in sugar levels.*

YPERINSULINISM

e consumption of carbohydrates and the
bsequent release of sugars into the blood
n provoke insulin levels to rise. This,
turn, causes blood sugar levels to fall.
nce blood sugars fall below a critical
vel, the brain, which needs glucose to
nction, demands more glucose. This dip
blood sugar is known as hypoglycaemia
low blood sugar.

The exaggerated insulin response caused
y the initial consumption of carbohydrates,
events the replenishment of sugars into
e blood stream that would usually restore
ood sugar levels. This is why a snack
gh in simple carbohydrates usually results
a downward energy dip soon afterwards
d a craving for more food.

Normally, when sugars are released into
e blood, the pancreas secretes the
ormone insulin into the bloodstream. The
sulin travels to the liver and to the muscle
ells, telling them to remove sugars from
e bloodstream and store it for future use.
yperinsulinism, or hyperinsulinemia,
escribes a condition in which much
o much insulin is being produced and
leased into the bloodstream, which then
mulates the liver and muscle cells to
move more glucose, resulting in hypogly-
aemia. This condition is thought to affect
s many as a quarter of the population.

When you eat carbohydrates, your
ody reacts by producing insulin, which
arries the sugar out of your bloodstream
to your cells. People who show a hyper
sponse produce too much insulin. They
ill be left with too little sugar in the
loodstream and too much stored in
ells as fat. This produces two problems:
eight gain and hypoglycaemia (low
ood sugar) with all its attendant
npleasant symptoms, such as dizziness,
weating and shaking.

WEIGHT GAIN

On a carefully controlled carbohydrate diet,
you should not gain weight as long as you
stick to healthy complex carbohydrates.
However, many people find that they are
unable to adequately burn up all the
carbohydrates that they consume, and any
excess is then inevitably stored as fat. It
is worth noting that, during exercise, the
body only begins to use up its reserves of
fat once all the carbohydrates consumed
have been used, and this often coincides
with the onset of fatigue.

Some people continue to gain weight or
simply maintain their weight no matter how
carefully they stick to their carbohydrate
diet. For them, the low-carbohydrate diet is
the best option. They are more likely to lose
weight steadily and healthily by sticking
to a low-carbohydrate diet containing
relatively high amounts of proteins and fats.

CHECKING FOR
HYPOGLYCAEMIA

There are a number of symptoms that
could indicate hypoglycaemia. Check
these out and then, if you are worried,
consult a medical practitioner. Do you
ever suffer from any of the following?

- ☐ tiredness and confusion
- ☐ dizziness and light-headedness
- ☐ sweating more than usual
- ☐ pale and tingly skin
- ☐ rapid heartbeat
- ☐ quick and shallow breathing
- ☐ trembling limbs
- ☐ feeling unusually hungry
- ☐ feeling irritable
- ☐ lack of co-ordination or clumsiness
- ☐ slurred speech

DIABETES

This disorder develops when the pancreas cannot produce enough insulin to cope with the amount of sugar in the blood or, in some instances, when it fails to produce any insulin at all. When insulin levels are low, the liver manufactures large amounts of glucose. The amount of sugar in the blood then increases above the normal level, while the levels in the body's tissues become inadequate.

Diabetes mellitus is the most common form of diabetes and, of the two types of diabetes mellitus, the second is the one that affects people over the age of 40 and those who are significantly overweight. Type I (insulin-dependent diabetes) occurs when the pancreas is unable to produce any insulin and so must be controlled by daily injections of insulin. It usually develops before the age of 30 and is the least common form of diabetes. Type II (non-insulin-dependent diabetes) accounts for some 90 per cent of all cases of diabetes and is a relatively common hazard from middle age onwards – which is why it is sometimes called late-onset diabetes. If Type II diabetes is not well managed, it can lead to heart disease, stroke and kidney failure. It can be controlled by diet, by

losing weight and by medication that stimulates the pancreas to produce more insulin. This is where the low-carbohydrate diet comes in. One of the great benefits of the low-carbohydrate diet is that the body

Above: *People suffering from diabetes need to monitor their blood sugar levels regularly because they are not able to produce enough insulin to manage the amounts of sugar effectively.*

will not be subjected to the great peaks and troughs of blood sugar levels that can occur when large amounts of carbohydrate are consumed, and this therefore lessens the risk of diabetes.

If you are diabetic, the liver is already producing large amounts of glucose, so the first thing you should cut from your diet is sugar, which many carbohydrates possess in abundance. The low-carbohydrate diet is therefore ideally suited to people with diabetes. This view is backed by many authorities who believe that a diet that is high in carbohydrates, particularly in refined white sugars and white flours and foods made from them such as cakes, biscuits (cookies), desserts, thick soups, potatoes, white rice and pasta, can lead to the development of Type II diabetes.

CHECKING FOR DIABETES

Many people do not realize that they are Type II diabetic until their symptoms gradually become more pronounced. Check out your symptoms.

❑ do you need to urinate frequently and copiously?
❑ do you experience excessive, unexplained thirst?
❑ do you suffer weight loss?
❑ do you feel weak and fatigued?

If you believe that you are diabetic, you should consult a doctor or health practitioner without delay and in the meantime cut out sugary foods.

If you are a diagnosed diabetic, you can test your blood sugar levels using a meter called a glucometer to check the amount of glucose in a drop of blood. Testing is usually done before or two hours after meals and at bedtime, although more frequent testing may be needed during times of illness or stress.

When the testing is carried out on a regular basis, it informs the diabetic person and his or her doctor how well diet, exercise and medication are working to control the diabetes. Meals, activity or medications can then be adjusted to keep blood sugar levels within a healthy range.

IGH BLOOD FAT LEVELS

you have high levels of blood fat – or
gh blood cholesterol – this could be
n early warning of heart disease. High
olesterol levels may lead to high blood
essure and to a number of heart disorders
nd diseases including heart attack.

It is important to have your cholesterol
vels checked professionally on a regular
asis from the age of 40 – and earlier
an that if there has been any previous
vidence of heart disease.

High blood fat levels can be affected by
hat you eat. Doubling or even tripling
ur intake of fresh vegetables and fruit,
utting out all salt and salty snacks such as
risps (US potato chips), and eating only
w-fat protein such as low-fat cheeses,
hicken and white fish may help.

High blood fat levels tend to be seen in
mokers more often than in non-smokers so
is important for smokers to quit the habit.

*elow: Eating too many of the wrong types
f carbohydrate can result in feelings of
omplete exhaustion.*

DIGESTIVE SYSTEM DISORDERS

For people with disorders of the digestive
system, such as diarrhoea, stomach cramps,
irritable bowel syndrome or diverticulitis,
a high-carbohydrate diet may prove too
stimulating to the system. For example,
muesli (granola) is a source of healthy
complex carbohydrates but, for some
people, it is too abrasive and results in
explosive diarrhoea and flatulence. For
them, the low-carbohydrate diet provides
a much gentler, healthier solution.

CHRONIC FATIGUE

If you are tired all the time, this may well
be a result of excess insulin and dipping
blood sugar levels and a diet that is too
high in carbohydrate and not high enough
in proteins, fats, and fruit and vegetables.

Fatigue can also be caused by drinking
too much alcohol, smoking, not drinking
enough water, stress, overwork, relationship
difficulties, money problems, pregnancy
and too little exercise. If fatigue persists,
even when you have made good lifestyle
choices, consult a medical practitioner.

CHECKING FOR CARBOHYDRATE ADDICTION

There are a number of symptoms that
can indicate carbohydrate addiction.
Check out your symptoms.

☐ do you become tired and/or
   hungry in the mid-afternoon?
☐ do you want more dessert within
   an hour of eating a large meal
   with a dessert?
☐ do you find eating breakfast makes
   it harder to stay on the diet?
☐ do you find it easier not to eat at all
   rather than simply cut down?
☐ do you have difficulty in eliminating
   starches from your diet?
☐ do you find that sweets (candies)
   and chocolate improve your mood?
☐ do you often not bother with
   vegetables or salad?
☐ do you experience a sleepy,
   drugged feeling after a large,
   starchy meal?
☐ do you like to have a snack just
   before bedtime?
☐ do you eat in the middle of
   the night?

If you find that you experience a number
of these symptoms, you may be showing
signs of carbohydrate addiction. If this
is the case, it may be the time for you
to make significant changes to your
diet. Your first step should be to cut
out sugar, white rice, pasta, potatoes,
bread, cakes, biscuits (cookies),
chocolate and alcohol.

CARBOHYDRATE ADDICTION

Some people become seriously addicted
to carbohydrate. It is thought that this is the
consequence of an excess of insulin. Until
relatively recently, insulin was most often
associated with diabetes, which is how
it was first identified. More up-to-date
research shows that it may be the key
hormone in regulating a great deal of
what we refer to as the metabolism.

the benefits of a low-carbohydrate diet

THE IMPORTANCE OF A BALANCED diet cannot be over-emphasized. What is most desirable is a good mix of foods including healthy carbohydrates, fats and proteins. On a low-carbohydrate diet you will redress the balance of foods you eat to promote optimum health and weight-loss.

A low-carbohydrate diet helps you to boost muscle mass and burn body fat so that you can achieve sustainable weight loss. When you first start to follow the diet, your weight may stay the same or even rise slightly. As long as you are not cheating with your diet, you can rest assured that this lack of weight loss is because you are building and strengthening your muscles – which weigh more than body fat. In time, you will find that your health, strength and stamina improve and you will be less tired.

EASY TO FOLLOW
The low-carbohydrate diet offers a huge freedom of choice, which makes it easy to follow and stick to. There is an extensive range of foods from which to choose, and this means that you can follow it even when eating out at a restaurant or staying with friends. Diets that are very restrictive soon fail when real life intervenes and can make going out or cooking and preparing food for a family a nightmare. This can often lead to an early abandonment of the diet.

IMPROVING HEALTH AND LOSING WEIGHT
Many of us become overly concerned with losing weight or body mass when it would be better to focus on re-educating the palate and setting a diet for life. What really matte in dieting terms is the ability and the will to sustain good eating habits permanently.

It is now well known that yo-yo dieting – the repetitive cycle of losing and gaining weight – upsets the body's natural control mechanisms, disrupts the body's appestat (the neural control centre within the brain that regulates the sense of hunger and satiety), creates insatiable cravings and can make us dangerously obsessed with losing weight. Rather than setting unrealistic weigh loss targets, it is much healthier to aim at losing no more than 450–900g/1–2lb a week, resulting in a total loss of about 34kg 75lb at most during one year. This is the lev of weight loss that can be comfortably sustained, while at the same time training yourself into new healthy eating habits.

THE END OF CRAVINGS
Many authorities now consider that eating carbohydrates can set up addiction in sor people and the more carbohydrate they eat, the more their bodies crave it. Following a low-carbohydrate diet can he to end the physical cravings that may be caused by carbohydrates, especially the "bad" carbohydrates. It can also help to er psychological cravings, once healthy eatin patterns are firmly established.

Left: *A low-carbohydrate diet allows you to eat a huge selection of different foods, making it easy and enjoyable to follow.*

Above: *Following a low-carbohydrate diet and excluding foods containing yeast such as bread and yeast extract may help to prevent recurrent yeast infections.*

PREVENTING YEAST INFECTIONS

Some women find that candida and other yeast-based disorders are decreased or even prevented once they start following a low-carbohydrate diet. If you repeatedly suffer with thrush, you will probably find it helpful to eliminate yeast-based products and increase your intake of live yogurt.

SIMPLE FOODS

Some nutritionists believe that we should only eat carbohydrate foods that can be eaten raw, claiming that concentrated carbohydrate sources, such as grains and grain products, should be excluded from the diet as human beings were never genetically programmed to eat these foods. It is a benefit of the low-carbohydrate diet that you could, if you wished, eat most of the allowed foods in their raw state. Because some vitamins are destroyed by cooking, eating raw vegetables, salads and fruit is especially good for us.

Right: *Following a low-carbohydrate diet with plenty of complex carbohydrates such as fresh vegetables will help you to establish healthy eating habits and end physical and psychological food cravings.*

DRINKING ENOUGH WATER

For optimum health, it is essential to drink plenty of water and this is a key feature of the low-carbohydrate diet. We should all drink at least eight glasses of water every day and preferably more. Many authorities maintain that 2 litres/3½ pints/8¾ cups of water a day is necessary for good health. If you use this as a base, it is suggested that you drink an additional 250ml/8fl oz/1 cup for every 11.5kg/25lb you are over your ideal weight. Other medical authorities now suggest a basic standard of 25ml/1fl oz/1½ tbsp water for every 900g/2lb body weight.

Whichever method you choose, you should increase your normal intake of water during hot weather and when engaging in exercise or any physically strenuous activity. Keep some water with you all the time and sip it frequently.

If you drink mineral water, it is sensible to change the brand from time to time. The proportions of the minerals and even the minerals themselves vary from one brand to another and by switching types, you will avoid upsetting the body's natural balance.

Above: *To reap the full health benefits of a low-carbohydrate diet, it is important to drink at least eight glasses of water a day.*

Fatigue is one of the early warning signs of dehydration, which makes the body more vulnerable to infections and viruses and less able to fight them off. If you find that you are persistently tired, check how much water you are drinking and increase your intake if necessary.

eating the right foods

A LOW-CARBOHYDRATE DIET offers a perfect balance of proteins and complex carbohydrates while containing only moderate amounts of salt, fats and simple sugars. This easy-to-follow combination of foods supplies all the nutrients needed for optimum health.

It is simplest to divide the foods you need to eat on a low-carbohydrate diet into four basic categories. For good health, you need to consume a variety of foods from each of the four groups every day, plus at least eight glasses of water:

- Meat, poultry and fish, which contain rich supplies of protein.
- Dairy products, which contain protein, calcium and some carbohydrates.
- Nuts, beans, peas and lentils, which contain a combination of protein and complex carbohydrates.
- Wholegrains, vegetables, salad leaves and fruit, which contain both complex carbohydrates and fibre.

MEAT, POULTRY AND FISH

These foods contain rich supplies of protein, which is essential for building new body tissue and supplying amino acids – small units of protein that repair old tissue. Protein builds and maintains bone, muscle, skin, hair and nails and is vital to the production of the hormones and enzymes that keep the body functioning properly.

You need to eat protein regularly because it cannot be stored in the body. However, many people consume twice as much protein than is actually needed and the excess is stored as fat. For good health, you only need to eat 65g/2½oz protein a day – this is equivalent to a chicken breast portion or a small portion of tuna fish.

The trouble with many sources of protein that come from animal produce is that they are high in unhealthy saturated fats, which can raise cholesterol levels in the blood. High cholesterol levels are associated with heart disease and should therefore be avoided. When choosing meat and poultry opt for lean cuts such as strips of beef fillet or chicken breast portions. Avoid eating too much red meat – one serving a week is ample for good health.

Fish and shellfish make a healthy, low-fat protein choice. Try to eat oily fish such as mackerel, sardines and trout at least once a week. They provide a rich supply of essential fatty acids, which are vital for good health.

DAIRY PRODUCTS

These foods, which include milk, yogurt, cheese, butter and eggs can, like animal protein, be high in saturated fats. Over the last few years, much has been written about the dangers of eating dairy products, and many people now routinely avoid them. However, this extreme measure can be a mistake. The nutrients found in dairy foods which include protein and calcium, are needed for health. The following guidelines should help you plan a balanced diet.
Milk Always choose skimmed or semi-skimmed (low-fat) milk rather than full-fat (whole) milk.
Yogurt Choose natural (plain) yogurt. If you prefer fruit-flavoured yogurt, stir in a little chopped or puréed fruit. This is a much healthier alternative than yogurts sweetened with refined sugar.

Left: *Lean meat, fish and shellfish offer a valuable source of low-fat protein. You should try to eat foods from this group, which also includes poultry, every day.*

NUTS, BEANS, PEAS AND LENTILS

These foods offer a valuable combination of complex carbohydrates, low-fat proteins, fibre and other essential nutrients including B vitamins, folic acid and iron. They play an important part in a varied and balanced diet, and foods from this group should be included in your daily diet. However, as nuts, beans, peas and lentils are relatively high in carbohydrates, they should comprise no more than 20 per cent of the total food consumed in a day.

The carbohydrates are absorbed slowly into the body, offering sustained energy that will not result in a sudden rush of sugars into the blood followed by an exaggerated release of insulin. The fibre provided by these foods is also essential to good health.

Left: You should eat a small quantity of nuts, beans, peas or lentils every day. They provide a healthy supply of complex carbohydrates that are absorbed slowly into the system.

heeses Cream cheeses and hard cheeses e high in saturated fats and should be aten only in moderation. Low-fat cheeses ch as cottage cheese or Quark make a ealthier choice.

utter This is high in saturated animal fats nd should be eaten only in moderation. ow-fat spreads, particularly those made ith mono-unsaturated olive oil, are a much ealthier choice.

ggs Do not eat more than six eggs a eek. Always choose a healthy cooking ethod such as boiling or poaching rather an frying. (It is interesting to note that e body uses up more calories digesting boiled egg than are actually provided y the egg itself – which gives boiled eggs useful place in any diet.)

ight: Dairy products such as milk, yogurt, ream and cheese are valuable sources f calcium, which is needed for healthy ones. Eggs are also included as dairy roducts. You should eat at least one ortion of this food group every day.

CHOOSING THE RIGHT CARBOHYDRATES

All carbohydrates are not the same and it can be difficult to know which ones to eat and which to avoid. The list below breaks them down into simple groups.

Green leafy vegetables such as spinach and lettuce and non-starchy vegetables such as cauliflower and broccoli contain small amounts of carbohydrate. You need to eat lots of these every day.

Non-starchy fruits and sweet-tasting vegetables such as carrots, beetroot (beets), squash and (bell) peppers contain higher levels of carbohydrate. Eat in moderation.

Wholegrains, beans and peas such as brown rice, kidney beans and chickpeas contain higher levels of carbohydrates but these are released slowly into the body, providing sustained energy. These should make up no more than 20 per cent of total food consumed.

Starchy vegetables and fruits such as yams, potatoes and bananas contain large amounts of quickly absorbed carbohydrates and must be avoided.

Foods containing sugar or refined flour such as cakes, white pasta and white bread are high in "bad" carbohydrates and must be avoided.

GRAINS, VEGETABLES, SALAD LEAVES AND FRUIT

These foods contain complex carbohydrates, healthy quantities of fibre and valuable supplies of vitamins and minerals.

Starchy grains Wholegrains supply fibre and complex carbohydrates, which provide the body with a good source of sustained energy. However, they should be eaten in moderation as they contain considerable amounts of carbohydrates.

Above: *Non-starchy vegetables and wholegrains such as barley provide complex carbohydrates and a valuable source of nutrients.*

Vegetables These can be divided into two categories – starchy vegetables and non-starchy vegetables. Starchy vegetables such as potatoes and yams are very high in quickly absorbed carbohydrates and should be avoided. Non-starchy vegetables such as broccoli, spinach, mushrooms and fennel contain smaller amounts of slowly-absorbed complex carbohydrate and should be eaten every day. (Sweet-tasting vegetables such as carrots contain higher levels of carbohydrate and should be eaten in moderation.)

Salad leaves These contain small amounts of carbohydrate should be eaten every day.

Fruit Starchy fruits such as bananas should be avoided. Non-starchy fruits such as grapefruit, plums and cherries can be eaten in moderation. Fruit contains natural sugars that add to its total carbohydrate content. Avoid very "sugary" fruits such as grapes.

Left: *When following a low-carbohydrate diet, eat at least one large salad every day*

avoiding the wrong foods

PEOPLE WERE NEVER DESIGNED to eat many of the foods that are available today. Because of this, the body accumulates unwelcome toxins and fat. Some of these contribute to furring up the arteries, causing headaches, kidney disease and weight-gain. Some foods can cause a combination of these problems.

n a low-carbohydrate diet, you need to oid starchy wholefoods such as potatoes, ms and bananas; refined carbohydrates ch as white rice, flour and sugar and ods made from them such as bread d pasta; and processed foods such as ocolate, crisps (US potato chips) and nvenience foods.

To obtain and maintain optimum health, u should cut out or cut down drastically the following foods and drinks:

sugar and foods containing sugar such sweets (candies), biscuits (cookies) and

low: Cut down or, better still, cut out kes, biscuits (cookies), sweet snacks and rbonated and sweetened drinks.

cakes • fried foods or pre-cooked, pre-packaged convenience foods and take-away meals • salt and salty snacks such as crisps and salted nuts • foods made from refined carbohydrates such as white bread and instant potato • breakfast cereals • sweetened drinks

AVOIDING STIMULANTS

You should also avoid stimulants. These are absorbed rapidly into the bloodstream, providing a quick energy fix but, because they have no nutritional value, the energy boost is soon replaced by a downward dip in blood sugar levels. Avoid the following:
• alcohol • caffeine (which can be found in tea, coffee, colas, chocolate and non-

prescription medicines such as cold and flu remedies) • cigarettes (smoke and tar from tobacco are among the most damaging substances that we can put into the body) • artificial sweeteners

LOW-CARBOHYDRATE TIPS

Check the label on packaged foods. While food labelling is useful, labels today can be so complicated that, if you're in a hurry, it can be difficult to read all the small print, make rapid calculations and decide on a purchase.

It is important to read the entire list of ingredients and not just pick out certain nutrients such as proteins or fats. Some apparently "light" products are certainly low in fat, but they may contain added sugar or more sugar than their "non-light" counterparts, increasing their carbohydrate content.
Eat less at meals. It can take a large amount of carbohydrate to make you feel full whereas proteins and fats are naturally more satisfying. After a few days on a low-carbohydrate diet, your body will start telling you that it is full sooner than expected and you should reduce your portion sizes accordingly. You will also find that you no longer feel the need to snack and resort to salty or sugary fillers between meals.
Take advantage of low-GIs and eat plenty of the foods that rate low on the glycaemic index. They have two key advantages for people who want to lose weight: they fill you up and keep you satisfied for longer because they are absorbed more slowly and they help you burn more of your body fat and less of your body muscle.

planning your menu

THE MAIN RULE TO FOLLOW on a low-carbohydrate diet is to keep your intake of carbohydrates low. There is no need to cut out carbohydrate altogether, and in fact, to do so would be unwise, because good carbohydrates are an essential part of a healthy, well-balanced diet.

As a basic guideline when planning your daily meals, try to make sure that starchy carbohydrates, such as brown rice and wholegrains, make up no more than 20 per cent of each meal. In simple terms this means that the food on your plate, no more than one-fifth of it should be starchy carbohydrates. The rest should be made up of low-fat protein, such as grilled (broiled) fish, and green leafy vegetables.

The essential elements of a healthy low-carbohydrate diet focus not only on the foods that you eat, but also on how and when you eat them. Keeping the body in good repair and with maximum energy levels depends on these factors. Make sure that you always:

- eat regularly, at about the same time each day
- make time to eat a sustaining breakfast
- have a healthy lunch
- eat a light dinner such as white meat or fish with salad

Above: *A sustaining breakfast such as a boiled egg and grilled bacon is a good start to a low-carbohydrate day.*

BREAKFAST

Start the day with a cup of boiling water with a slice of lemon. If you like to have a cup of tea or coffee with your breakfast, choose a decaffeinated variety and drink a glass of water as well. For your meal, always choose substantial, high-protein, low-carbohydrate foods that will set you up for the day. Choose dishes such as:

- grilled (broiled) bacon and a boiled or poached egg
- scrambled or boiled egg
- poached haddock
- cheese on a very thin slice of wholegrain bread
- slices of cold ham and cheese
- kippers (smoked herrings)
- tomatoes and mushrooms on a very thin slice of wholegrain toast

SNACKS

Mid-morning, drink a glass of water and, if you are hungry, eat a piece of fruit, such as an apple or orange (avoid bananas as they are starchy and high in carbohydrate), or a small pot of natural (plain) yogurt. Raw vegetables such as sticks of carrot and cucumber also make a good snack.

Sweet snacks, cakes, cookies and crisps (US potato chips) have no place in the low-carbohydrate diet. They contain very few health-providing nutrients and are very high in carbohydrates. Because of the high sugar content in sweet snacks such as biscuits (cookies), your body will start to crave these foods the more you eat them.

As your body becomes attuned to eating less carbohydrate and more protein, fat and fruit and vegetables, you will start to find that you have less need for snacks and coffee break treats. Breakfast is likely to keep you going through the morning.

THE IMPORTANCE OF WATER

It is essential to drink water in order to fight off the possible side effects of a low-carbohydrate diet, which can include constipation, bad breath and irritable bowel syndrome (characterized by bloating, cramps and diarrhoea, alternating with constipation). Water greatly aids the digestive processes, helps to eliminate toxins from the system and helps to prevent constipation, bloating and fatigue.

Every day drink at least the minimum recommendation of eight glasses of water, and more if you also drink tea, coffee or alcohol, all of which can dehydrate the body. Start the day well by drinking either a glass of water or a glass of boiled water with a slice of lemon in order to aid digestion.

Above: *Fruit, such as an apple or orange, makes a good mid-morning snack, but avoid high-carbohydrate bananas.*

Choose dishes such as:

- light home-made soups (do not thicken them with flour or potato)
- grilled (broiled) fish served with steamed broccoli or spinach
- stir-fried vegetables with tofu or strips of lean meat
- a large leaf salad with a poached egg
- an omelette with a large leaf salad

ove: *A large leafy salad served with es of grilled chicken makes a satisfying, lthy, low-carbohydrate lunch.*

Above: *Strips of mixed raw vegetables are low in carbohydrates and packed with healthy nutrients, so make a good snack.*

Vegetarians If you are a vegetarian, you need to reduce the amount of wholemeal (whole-wheat) breads and pastas that you eat, while at the same time increasing the amount of cheeses, eggs, vegetables, salads, fruits, nuts and pulses.

NCH

er a substantial breakfast, you will need y a light lunch accompanied by a glass water. Eating lightly will also help vent you from becoming tired in the rnoon. Choose such dishes as:

a large mixed salad with canned sardines
a large mixed salad with strips of grilled (broiled) chicken
courgette (zucchini), tomato and chickpea salad
tomato, olive and onion salad with a little crumbled feta cheese

Sandwiches These aren't an ideal choice on a low-carbohydrate diet. However, if they cannot be avoided, some types of sandwich can make a better choice than others. Avoid large filled rolls and heavy breads, such as rye bread, because of their high carbohydrate content. Instead choose thinly sliced wholemeal bread. Fillings can include sliced hard-boiled egg, salads, tuna (mixed with a little natural [plain] yogurt), yeast extract and slices of cucumber, chicken, crab meat, roast beef, pastrami or sardines. If you do eat a sandwich, always drink two glasses of water with it.

Eating with friends and family Never let yourself become a slave to any diet. It is far better to enjoy yourself whether you are at home or out, and this is very easy with a low-carbohydrate diet. It is simple to decline potatoes, breads, rice and any foods that contain refined white sugar and white flour, and help yourself to more of the other foods that are on offer.

DINNER

After a sustaining breakfast and a healthy lunch, the evening meal can be light. This is best for health and the body's digestive system. You can choose whatever you like from the four food groups, provided that you keep carbohydrate to no more than 20 per cent of the total foods that you eat. Remember to drink a couple of glasses of water during the evening.

Foods that you eat during the day are more likely to be burned off. However, food that you eat in the evening is more likely to be stored as body fat. The way to avoid this happening is to eat early in the evening and then take some exercise later. You could take a trip to the gym, go swimming (which is a good way of relaxing before going to sleep) or go for a good walk.

ove: *Sandwiches should be avoided – if they are the only choice, choose one h thinly sliced wholegrain bread.*

improving your lifestyle for health

HOWEVER HEALTHY AND WELL-BALANCED your diet, you need to maintain a healthy lifestyle, too, to make sure that yo body stays in optimum condition. It is important to address unhealthy habits such as smoking or over-indulging in alcohol and consider other factors such as exercise and reducing stre

GENERAL HEALTH CHECKLIST

There are several common warning signs that can indicate poor health. If you suffer from the following, consul a medical practitioner.

- ☐ feeling tired in the morning when you wake up
- ☐ feeling irritable
- ☐ aching muscles and joints, including aching legs
- ☐ shortness of breath upon climbing stairs
- ☐ inability to run
- ☐ recurrent headache and stomach ache
- ☐ fluid retention (oedema)
- ☐ swelling in the joints, especially at hip and knee
- ☐ back problems
- ☐ indigestion
- ☐ constipation

Left: *Going for a bicycle ride in the fres air is not only healthy exercise but can reduce stress levels at the same time.*

GIVING UP SMOKING

If you smoke, the single most important step you can take for your health is to give up. Tobacco smoke can cause serious damage to every system of the body and result in potentially fatal conditions. There is really no easy way to give up smoking. You simply have to resolve to do so and then just stop. Some people find using nicotine patches or nicotine gum useful to help alleviate any withdrawal symptoms and others find the support of a self-help group encourages them to stop.

CUTTING DOWN ON ALCOHOL

Moderation is the keyword when talking about alcohol. Alcohol in excess stimulates and depresses the nervous system and steadily damages the liver, pancreas and vital organs of the body over a period of years, and causes dehydration.

A glass of wine or beer is thought not to damage your health and is even thought by some to have health benefits. However, alcoholic drinks tend to be quite high in carbohydrates so should be avoided or restricted on a low-carbohydrate diet.

SLEEP, EXERCISE AND STRES REDUCTION

Good general health depends not only what and how you eat, but also, most importantly, on the opportunities you giv your body to repair and renew itself. Ce regeneration cannot take place if you ar always over-tired, sedentary and stresse

Good sleep Although it is not always possible, it is best to go to sleep at abou the same time every night and get up at about the same time each morning, rathe than vary your sleeping hours wildly. A ood, regular sleeping pattern encourages ou to sleep, helping you to overcome any roblems of insomnia, and is more likely to oduce a truly refreshing and restorative eep. The body welcomes regular habits.

Make sure that your bed is comfortable nd supportive. If it is soft and spongy r more than ten years old, it is time to place it. The bedroom should be well entilated with a partly open window, and ee of distractions such as a computer, elevision, books and newspapers.

aking exercise Everyone needs to exercise t least three times a week for 30 minutes ach time. Choose whichever form of xercise appeals to you and which is onsistent with your present levels of fitness. Many people find that walking and/or wimming is by far the best all-round form f exercise. Walking can very easily be ncorporated into your normal lifestyle with ery little disruption. You may consider valking to work instead of taking the car or he bus, for example. Walk up stairs rather han taking a lift (elevator) or escalator. xercise classes, such as aerobics, yoga or ilates, and cycling are also good forms f exercise. Dancing is very healthy and an be fitted into your social life.

While a good minimum rule of thumb for xercise is 30 minutes three times a week, ll of us would benefit from more. As your tness levels increase, you can slowly ncrease the amount of exercise you take.

educing stress Most people have stresses n their lives and this can impact on their ealth. The key is to minimize them as far s possible, find positive ways of dealing vith difficult situations, and eliminate or esolve any situation that causes recurrent egative or long-term stress. Even if the ause of the stress is a problem that cannot e resolved – or, at least, not immediately – you can change your attitude towards it.

Think through all the various different spects of your life, such as your work, your relationships and your family, and pinpoint where the stresses lie. Some situations can be resolved through radical action, while others can at least be mproved. No one should have to tolerate

Above: *Practising a relaxation technique such as meditation can be invaluable in reducing your stress levels.*

long-lasting stressful or hurtful situations: it is up to you to take the necessary steps to reduce the stresses in your life and in so doing improve your overall health.

Exercise such as yoga or tai chi and relaxation techniques such as meditation can often help to reduce stress levels. Taking time to yourself is very important. If necessary, seek professional help, rather than struggle on alone.

IMPROVING YOUR HEALTH THROUGH DIET

The following pages provide you with recipes that will help you follow a healthy lifestyle through diet. Remember this is as much a diet designed to help you lose weight as one geared for maximum energy and the optimum quality of life.

COOKING FOR HEALTH

As well as eating healthy foods, you need to prepare them in a healthy way. The following four cooking methods are perfect for a healthy low-carbohydrate diet as they use little or no fat and help to preserve water-soluble nutrients that can easily be lost by other cooking methods, such as boiling. They also give delicious results.

Steaming is a good cooking method for fish and vegetables.
Microwaving is similar to steaming and is good for fish and vegetables.
Grilling (broiling) is a particularly good cooking method for meat, poultry, fish and vegetables such as aubergines (eggplant) and (bell) peppers.
Baking is particularly good for fish, vegetables and fruit.

breakfasts

FOR GOOD HEALTH, A SUSTAINING breakfast is an essential start to the day. Many classic breakfast foods such as cereal or bagels, which can contain over 35g of carbohydrate per serving, are not an option on a low-carbohydrate diet. However, there are lots of other quick, simple and nutritious choices that are just as tasty. Eggs are a popular breakfast dish, and they can be served in a variety of delicious ways. Make the most of weekend mornings, by taking the time to prepare and enjoy a leisurely breakfast of poached eggs Florentine or herrings in oatmeal with bacon.

griddled tomatoes on toast

LITTLE COULD BE SIMPLER and tastier than this breakfast dish. Tomatoes are rich in vitamin C and the thinly sliced wholegrain toast provides fibre and slowly-absorbed complex carbohydrate.

1 Brush a ridged griddle pan with a little olive oil and heat. Lay the slices of tomato on the pan and cook for about 4 minutes, turning once.

2 Meanwhile, lightly toast the thin slices of wholegrain bread. Place the tomatoes on top. Drizzle the tomatoes with a little olive oil and balsamic vinegar. Season with salt and pepper and serve with shavings of Parmesan cheese, if you like.

Serves 4

olive oil, for brushing
  and drizzling
6 tomatoes, thickly sliced
4 thin slices wholegrain bread
balsamic vinegar, for drizzling
salt and ground black pepper
shavings of Parmesan cheese,
  to serve (optional)

COOK'S TIPS

• To reduce the total amount of carbohydrate in this dish, try to cut the bread as thinly as possible.
• Using a ridged griddle pan reduces the amount of oil required for cooking and imparts the smoky flavour of foods that have been cooked on a barbecue.

NUTRITION NOTES

Per portion:	
Energy	105Kcal/438kJ
Protein	3.2g
Fat	3.8g
saturated fat	0.65g
Carbohydrate	15.5g
Fibre	2.4g
Calcium	28.2mg

savoury scrambled eggs

HIGH IN PROTEIN and low in carbohydrate, these tasty scrambled eggs will make a nutritious breakfast that will keep you going throughout the morning.

erves 2

slices wholegrain bread
5g/1oz/2 tbsp butter
eggs and 2 egg yolks, beaten
0–90ml/4–6 tbsp semi-skimmed
(low-fat) milk
alt and ground black pepper
nchovy fillets, cut into strips, and paprika,
to garnish
nchovy paste, such as Gentleman's Relish,
for spreading

1 Toast the bread, then remove the crusts and cut the toast into triangles or squares, you like. Keep warm.

2 Meanwhile, melt the butter in a pan over a very low heat.

3 Pour the eggs and milk into the butter and stir in a little salt and pepper. Heat very gently, stirring constantly, until the mixture begins to thicken. Remove the pan from the heat and continue to stir until the mixture becomes very creamy.

4 Place the toast on two plates and divide the eggs equally among them. Garnish each portion with strips of anchovy fillet and a generous sprinkling of paprika. Serve immediately, with anchovy paste to spread on the toast.

NUTRITION NOTES

Per portion:	
Energy	220Kcal/919kJ
Protein	13.7g
Fat	13.3g
saturated fat	3.8g
Carbohydrate	13g
Fibre	1.1g
Calcium	112mg

poached eggs florentine

THE CLASSIC COMBINATION of eggs and spinach is high in protein and packed with vitamins and minerals. It is tasty and sustaining and makes an ideal weekend brunch if you have an active day ahead of you.

Serves 4
675g/1½lb spinach, washed
    and drained
pinch of freshly grated nutmeg

For the topping
25g/1oz/2 tbsp butter
25g/1oz/¼ cup plain (all-purpose) flour
300ml/½ pint/1¼ cups hot milk
pinch of ground mace
115g/4oz/1 cup grated Gruyère cheese
4 eggs
15ml/1 tbsp freshly grated Parmesan
    cheese, plus shavings to garnish
salt and ground black pepper

VARIATION
To make a low-fat version of this dish, omit the Gruyère cheese from the sauce and topping. It will work just as well.

1 Preheat the oven to 200°C/400°F/ Gas 6. Place the spinach in a large pan with a little water. Cook for 3–4 minutes, then drain well and chop finely.

2 Return the spinach to the pan, add the nutmeg and seasoning and heat through. Spoon into four small gratin dishes, making a well in the middle of each.

3 To make the topping, melt the butter in a small pan, add the flour and cook for 1 minute, stirring constantly. Gradually blend in the hot milk, beating well. Cook for 2 minutes, stirring constantly. Remove from the heat and stir in the mace and 75g/3oz/¾ cup of the Gruyère cheese.

4 Break each egg into a cup and slide into a pan of lightly salted simmering water. Poach for 3–4 minutes. Lift the eggs out using a slotted spoon and drain on kitchen paper.

5 Place a poached egg in the middle of each dish and cover with the sauce. Sprinkle with the remaining cheeses and bake for 10 minutes, or until just golden. Garnish with shavings of Parmesan cheese and serve immediately.

NUTRITION NOTES

Per portion:	
Energy	366Kcal/1404kJ
Protein	25.9g
Fat	24.8g
saturated fat	12.4g
Carbohydrate	11.3g
Fibre	3.7g
Calcium	747mg

omelette arnold bennett

A CREAMY, SMOKED HADDOCK soufflé omelette is low in carbohydrate and perfect for a leisurely weekend breakfast. Fish is an excellent source of protein, but the cream, butter and cheese make it high in fat so save it for a special occasion.

3 Mix the egg yolks with 15ml/1 tbsp of the remaining cream. Season, then stir into the fish. In a separate bowl, combine the cheese and remaining cream.

4 Whisk the egg whites until stiff, then fold into the fish mixture. Heat the remaining butter in an omelette pan, add the fish mixture and cook until browned underneath. Pour the cheese mixture over and grill (broil) until bubbling. Garnish with watercress and serve.

COOK'S TIP
Try to buy smoked haddock that does not contain artificial colouring for this recipe. Apart from being better for you, it gives the omelette a lighter, more attractive colour.

NUTRITION NOTES

Per portion:	
Energy	429Kcal/1795kJ
Protein	15g
Fat	40.5g
saturated fat	24.7g
Carbohydrate	1.7g
Fibre	0g
Calcium	125.5mg

Serves 4

175g/6oz smoked haddock fillet, poached and drained
50g/2oz/4 tbsp butter, diced
175ml/6fl oz/¾ cup whipping cream
4 eggs, separated
40g/1½oz/⅓ cup mature (sharp) Cheddar cheese, grated
ground black pepper
watercress, to garnish

1 Remove and discard the skin from the haddock fillet. If there are any small bones remaining, remove them with tweezers and discard, then carefully flake the flesh using a fork.

2 Melt half the butter with 60ml/4 tbsp of the cream in a non-stick pan, then stir in the flaked fish. Cover and set aside to cool. Preheat the grill (broiler).

soufflé omelette with mushrooms

A LIGHT, MOUTHWATERING omelette makes a great morning meal. Mushrooms contain barely any carbohydrate, but are wonderfully satisfying and a source of B vitamins and minerals.

Serves 2

2 eggs, separated
15g/½oz/1 tbsp butter
flat leaf parsley or coriander (cilantro)
　leaves, to garnish

For the mushroom sauce
15g/½oz/1 tbsp butter
75g/3oz/generous 1 cup button (white)
　mushrooms, thinly sliced
15ml/1 tbsp plain (all-purpose) flour
75–120ml/2½–4fl oz/⅓–½ cup milk
5ml/1 tsp chopped fresh
　parsley (optional)
salt and ground black pepper

2 Stir the flour into the mushrooms, then slowly add the milk, stirring constantly. Bring to the boil and cook until thickened. Add the parsley, if using, and season with salt and pepper to taste. Keep warm.

3 Beat the egg yolks with 15ml/1 tbsp water and season with a little salt and pepper. Whisk the egg whites until stiff, then fold into the egg yolks using a metal spoon. Preheat the grill (broiler).

4 Melt the butter in a large frying pan and pour the egg mixture into the pan. Cook over a gentle heat for 2–3 minutes. Place the frying pan under the grill and cook for a further 2–3 minutes, until the top is golden brown.

5 Pour the mushroom sauce over the top of the omelette and fold it in half. Cut the omelette in half, and slide each portion on to a warmed plate. Serve immediately, garnished with parsley or coriander leaves

1 First, make the mushroom sauce. Melt the butter in a frying pan and add the sliced mushrooms. Cook gently over a low heat, stirring occasionally, for 4–5 minutes, until tender and juicy.

NUTRITION NOTES

Per portion:

Energy	244Kcal/1020kJ
Protein	10.6g
Fat	17.5g
saturated fat	10.4g
Carbohydrate	8.5g
Fibre	0.7g
Calcium	106.4mg

stuffed thai omelettes

LOW IN CARBOHYDRATE and saturated fat, these omelettes'
subtle combination of fragrant coriander and hot chilli will
instantly invigorate and kick-start a sluggish system.

rves 4

)ml/2 tbsp vegetable oil
garlic cloves, finely chopped
small onion, finely chopped
25g/8oz/2 cups minced (ground) pork
)ml/2 tbsp Thai fish sauce
tomatoes, peeled and chopped
5ml/1 tbsp chopped fresh
coriander (cilantro)
ound black pepper
rigs of coriander (cilantro) and red
chillies, thinly sliced, to garnish

r the omelettes
-6 eggs
5ml/1 tbsp Thai fish sauce
)ml/2 tbsp vegetable oil

Heat the oil in a wok, add the garlic and
onion, and cook for 3–4 minutes, until
ft. Add the pork and cook, stirring, for
out 8 minutes until lightly browned.

) Stir the fish sauce, tomatoes and
 pepper into the pork; simmer until
ghtly thickened. Mix in the coriander.

 To make the omelettes, whisk the eggs
 and fish sauce together. Heat 15ml/
tbsp of the oil in an omelette pan or wok.
dd half the beaten egg mixture and tilt the
n to spread the egg into an even shape.

 Cook until the omelette is just set, then
 spoon half the filling into the centre.
ld into a neat square parcel by bringing
e opposite sides of the omelette towards
ch other – first the top and bottom, then
e right and left sides.

COOK'S TIP
For a milder flavour, discard the seeds
and membrane of the chillies because
this is where most of their heat resides.

5 Carefully slide the parcel on to a
 warmed serving dish, folded side
down and keep warm. Make a second
omelette parcel with the remaining oil,
eggs and filling and slide it on to the
serving dish.

6 Cut each omelette parcel in half, and
 serve immediately garnished with
sprigs of fresh coriander and thinly sliced
red chillies.

NUTRITION NOTES

Per portion:	
Energy	309Kcal/1291kJ
Protein	23.4g
Fat	22.8g
saturated fat	4.5g
Carbohydrate	4.1g
Fibre	0.9g
Calcium	63.8mg

herrings in oatmeal with bacon

OILY FISH ARE AN EXCELLENT SOURCE of omega-3 fatty acids, which are essential for good health. They make a delicious, sustaining breakfast to take you through the day. For extra colour and flavour, serve with grilled tomatoes.

Serves 4

50g/2oz/½ cup medium oatmeal
10ml/2 tsp mustard powder
4 herrings, about 225g/8oz each,
　cleaned, boned, heads and tails removed
30ml/2 tbsp sunflower oil
8 rindless bacon rashers (strips)
salt and ground black pepper
lemon wedges, to serve

1 In a shallow dish, combine the oatmeal and mustard powder and season. Press the herrings in the mixture to coat.

2 Heat the oil in a large frying pan and fry the bacon until crisp. Drain on kitchen paper and keep hot.

3 Gently lay the herrings into the pan. You may need to cook them in two batches to avoid overcrowding the pan. Cook the fish for 3–4 minutes on each side, until crisp and golden.

4 Using a fish slice (metal spatula), lift the herrings from the pan and place on warmed serving plates with the streaky bacon rashers. Serve immediately with lemon wedges for squeezing over.

NUTRITION NOTES

Per portion:	
Energy	675Kcal/2821kJ
Protein	48.7g
Fat	46.9g
saturated fat	11.4g
Carbohydrate	10.5g
Fibre	1.9g
Calcium	146mg

devilled kidneys

THIS TRADITIONAL ENGLISH breakfast dish is a great way to start the day for anyone on a low-carbohydrate diet. It is packed with protein, low in fat and contains a negligible amount of carbohydrate.

Serves 4
25g/1oz/2 tbsp butter
1 shallot, finely chopped
2 garlic cloves, finely chopped
115g/4oz/1½ cups mushrooms, sliced
1.5ml/¼ tsp cayenne pepper
15ml/1 tbsp Worcestershire sauce
8 lamb's kidneys, halved and trimmed
30ml/2 tbsp chopped fresh parsley

COOK'S TIP
If you prefer not to eat spicy food first thing in the morning, omit the cayenne pepper. The dish will be just as tasty but milder on the palate.

1 Melt the butter in a frying pan, then add the shallots, garlic and mushrooms and cook for about 5 minutes. Stir in the cayenne pepper and Worcestershire sauce and cook for 1 minute more.

2 Add the kidneys to the pan and cook for 3–5 minutes on each side. Sprinkle with chopped parsley, divide among warm serving plates and serve immediately.

NUTRITION NOTES

Per portion:

Energy	190Kcal/794kJ
Protein	31.2g
Fat	7.3g
saturated fat	3.3g
Carbohydrate	0.2g
Fibre	0.4g
Calcium	17.5mg

soups
and appetizers

LIGHT SOUPS, whether served as a first course or as a simple lunch, can work perfectly as part of a low-carbohydrate diet. They are quick and simple to prepare, making it easy to include them as an essential part of your eating plan. As well as soups, there are plenty of low-carbohydrate appetizers that you can enjoy without compromising on flavour or your diet.

thai fish soup

LIGHT AND AROMATIC – and with virtually no carbohydrate this is a perfect lunch or dinner dish. It is an excellent source of low-fat protein and contains essential nutrients for good health

Serves 2–3

1 litre/1¾ pints/4 cups fish stock
4 lemon grass stalks
3 limes
2 small fresh hot red chillies, seeded and
    thinly sliced
2cm/¾in piece fresh galangal, peeled and
    thinly sliced
6 coriander (cilantro) stalks, with leaves
2 kaffir lime leaves, coarsely
    chopped (optional)
350g/12oz monkfish fillet, skinned and cut
    into 2.5cm/1in pieces
15ml/1 tbsp rice vinegar
45ml/3 tbsp Thai fish sauce
30ml/2 tbsp chopped fresh coriander
    (cilantro) leaves, to garnish

1 Pour the stock into a large pan and bring
to the boil. Slice the bulb ends of the
lemon grass diagonally into 3mm/⅛in thick
pieces. Peel off four wide strips of lime rind
with a vegetable peeler, avoiding the white
pith. Squeeze the limes and reserve the juice.

2 Add the lemon grass, lime rind, chillies,
galangal and coriander stalks to the
stock, with the kaffir lime leaves, if using.
Simmer for 1–2 minutes.

3 Add the monkfish, vinegar, fish sauce
and half the reserved lime juice. Simmer
for 3 minutes, until the fish is just cooked.

4 Remove the coriander stalks from the
pan and discard. Taste the broth and
add more lime juice if necessary. Serve the
soup very hot, sprinkled with the chopped
coriander leaves.

VARIATION
Other fish or shellfish such as sole,
prawns (shrimp), scallops or squid can
be substituted for the monkfish.

NUTRITION NOTES

Per portion:	
Energy	116Kcal/484k
Protein	25.8g
Fat	0.7g
saturated fat	0.2g
Carbohydrate	0.1g
Fibre	0g
Calcium	17.4mg

miso broth with tofu

THIS FLAVOURSOME BROTH is simple and highly nutritious. In Japan, it is traditionally eaten for breakfast but it also makes a good appetizer, light lunch or supper.

rves 4

ounch of spring onions (scallions) or
5 baby leeks
5g/½oz fresh coriander (cilantro)
thin slices fresh root ginger
star anise
small dried red chilli
2 litres/2 pints/5 cups dashi or
vegetable stock
25g/8oz pak choi (bok choy) or other
Asian greens, thickly sliced
00g/7oz firm tofu, cut into 2.5cm/
1in cubes
0ml/4 tbsp red miso
0–45ml/2–3 tbsp Japanese soy sauce
fresh red chilli, seeded and
shredded (optional)

Cut the coarse green tops off the spring onions or baby leeks and slice the rest of e spring onions or leeks finely on the agonal. Place the coarse green tops in a rge pan with the stalks from the coriander, e fresh root ginger, star anise, dried chilli nd dashi or vegetable stock.

2 Heat the mixture over a low heat until boiling, then lower the heat and simmer r about 10 minutes. Strain the broth, return to the pan and reheat until simmering. Add e green portion of the sliced spring onions r leeks to the soup with the pak choi or sian greens and tofu. Cook for 2 minutes.

3 In a small bowl, combine the miso with a little soup, then stir the mixture into the pan. Add soy sauce to taste.

4 Coarsely chop the coriander leaves and stir most of them into the soup with the white part of the spring onions or leeks. Cook for 1 minute, then ladle the soup into warmed bowls. Sprinkle with the remaining chopped coriander and the shredded fresh red chilli, if using, and serve immediately.

NUTRITION NOTES

Per portion:	
Energy	72Kcal/300kJ
Protein	7.2g
Fat	3.1g
saturated fat	0.4g
Carbohydrate	4.2g
Fibre	3.4g
Calcium	374mg

hot and sour soup

THE HERBS, SPICES AND AROMATICS in this light and health
soup provide a useful supply of nutrients and phytochemicals to
help promote good health.

Serves 6

225g/8oz unpeeled raw prawns (shrimp)
2 lemon grass stalks
1.5 litres/2½ pints/6¼ cups
    vegetable stock
4 kaffir lime leaves
2 slices peeled fresh root ginger
60ml/4 tbsp Thai fish sauce
60ml/4 tbsp fresh lime juice
2 garlic cloves, crushed
6 spring onions (scallions), chopped
1 fresh red chilli, seeded and cut into strips
115g/4oz/generous 1½ cups oyster
    mushrooms, sliced
fresh coriander (cilantro) leaves and kaffir
    lime slices, to garnish

1 Peel the prawns and set them aside. Put the
shells in a large pan. Lightly crush the
lemon grass and add the stalks to the pan
with the stock, lime leaves and ginger.

NUTRITION NOTES

Per portion:

Energy	34Kcal/142kJ
Protein	7.2g
Fat	0.4g
saturated fat	0.07g
Carbohydrate	0.5g
Fibre	0.3g
Calcium	35.5mg

2 Bring the stock and aromatics to the
boil, then simmer for about 20 minutes.
Strain into a large, clean pan. Discard the
prawn shells, lime leaves and root ginger.

3 Add the Thai fish sauce, lime juice,
garlic, spring onions, chilli and sliced
oyster mushrooms to the stock. Bring the
mixture to the boil, lower the heat and simm
gently for 5 minutes.

4 Add the peeled prawns to the broth an
cook for 2–3 minutes. Serve
immediately, garnished with fresh coriander
leaves and slices of kaffir lime.

COOK'S TIP

Do not overcook the prawns or they will
become tough and chewy and spoil the
delicate nature of the soup.

ish and egg-knot soup

TWISTS OF OMELETTE and steamed prawn balls add protein and substance to this light Asian soup. It is the perfect appetizer before a low-carbohydrate main course.

rves 4

spring onion (scallion), finely shredded
)0ml/1½ pints/3½ cups well-flavoured
stock or dashi
nl/1 tsp soy sauce
ish of sake or dry white wine
nch of salt

r the prawn balls

)0g/7oz/generous 1 cup large raw
prawns (shrimp), peeled, thawed if frozen
5g/2½oz cod fillet, skinned
nl/1 tsp egg white
nl/1 tsp sake or dry white wine, plus
a dash extra
5ml/1½ tbsp cornflour (cornstarch) or
potato flour
–3 drops soy sauce
nch of salt

r the omelette

egg, beaten
ish of mirin
nch of salt
l, for cooking

To make the prawn balls, use a pin to
remove the black vein running down the
ack of each prawn. Place the prawns, cod,
gg white, sake or dry white wine, cornflour
r potato flour, soy sauce and a pinch of salt
a food processor or blender and process
a thick, sticky paste.

2 Shape the fish mixture into four balls,
place in a steaming basket and steam
over a pan of vigorously boiling water for
about 10 minutes.

3 Soak the shredded spring onion in iced
water for about 5 minutes, until the
shreds curl. Drain and set aside.

4 To make the omelette, combine the egg,
mirin and salt. Heat a little oil in a frying
pan and pour in the egg and mirin mixture,
coating the pan evenly. When the omelette
has set, turn it over and cook for 30 seconds.
Slide out and leave to cool, then cut the
omelette into strips and tie each in a knot.

5 Heat the stock or dashi, then add the
soy sauce, wine and salt. Divide the
prawn balls and egg-knots among four bowls
and add the soup. Serve with the onion curls.

NUTRITION NOTES

Per portion:	
Energy	94Kcal/392kJ
Protein	13.8g
Fat	2.3g
saturated fat	0.6g
Carbohydrate	5.3g
Fibre	0g
Calcium	53.9mg

quail's eggs in aspic with prosciutto

THESE PRETTY LITTLE EGGS in jelly are easy to make and great for summer dining. They are excellent served with mixed salad leaves, which won't add to the total carbohydrate content.

4 Rinse 12 dariole moulds, but do not dry then place the moulds on a tray. Cut each slice of ham in half and roll or fold so that they will fit into the moulds.

5 Place a coriander leaf flat in the base of each dariole mould, then put a peeled egg on top. As the jelly begins to thicken, spoon in enough to nearly cover each egg, holding the egg steady. Put a slice of ham on each egg and spoon in the rest of the jelly to fill the moulds.

6 Transfer the tray of moulds to a cool place and leave for 3–4 hours until set and cold. When ready to serve, run a rounded knife blade around the sides of the dariole moulds to loosen. Dip the moulds into warm water and tap gently until they become loose. Invert the eggs on to small plates and serve immediately.

Makes 12

22g packet aspic powder
45ml/3 tbsp dry sherry
12 quail's eggs or other small eggs
6 slices prosciutto
12 fresh coriander (cilantro) leaves

NUTRITION NOTES

Per portion:	
Energy	59Kcal/246kJ
Protein	6.5g
Fat	3.3g
saturated fat	1.0g
Carbohydrate	0.05g
Fibre	0g
Calcium	17.7mg

1 To make the aspic jelly, follow the instructions on the packet, but replace 45ml/3 tbsp of the recommended quantity of water with the dry sherry to give it a greater depth of flavour.

2 Cover the bowl of aspic jelly with clear film (plastic wrap) and place in the refrigerator until it is just beginning to thicken, but do not let it set or become too thick.

3 Meanwhile, put the eggs in a pan of cold water and bring to the boil. Boil for 1½ minutes, then pour off the hot water and leave the eggs to stand in a bowl of cold water until completely cool. This way, the yolks should still be a little soft, but the eggs will be firm enough to peel.

vegetable pancakes with tomato salsa

SPINACH AND EGG pancakes make a great start to a low-carbohydrate meal. Spinach offers a useful source of valuable nutrients such as vitamin C, folic acid and iron.

akes 10
25g/8oz spinach
small leek
few sprigs of fresh coriander (cilantro)
or parsley
large (US extra large) eggs
0g/2oz/½ cup plain (all-purpose)
flour, sifted
l, for frying
5g/1oz/½ cup freshly grated
Parmesan cheese
lt, ground black pepper and freshly
grated nutmeg

r the salsa
tomatoes, peeled and chopped
fresh red chilli, finely chopped
pieces sun-dried tomato in oil, drained
and chopped
small red onion, chopped
garlic clove, crushed
0ml/4 tbsp olive oil
0ml/2 tbsp sherry
.5ml/½ tsp soft light brown sugar

COOK'S TIP
Try to find sun-ripened tomatoes for the salsa, as these have the best and sweetest flavour and are much superior to those ripened under glass.

Prepare the tomato salsa. Place all the ingredients in a bowl and toss together to ombine. Cover and leave to stand in a cool lace for 2–3 hours.

2 To make the pancakes, finely shred or chop the spinach, leek and coriander or arsley. If you prefer, chop them in a food rocessor, but do not overprocess. Place the hopped vegetables in a bowl and beat in e eggs and seasoning. Blend in the flour nd 30–45ml/2–3 tbsp water and leave o stand for 20 minutes.

3 To cook the pancakes, drop spoonfuls of the batter into a lightly oiled frying pan and cook until golden underneath. Using a fish slice (metal spatula), turn the pancakes over and cook briefly on the other side.

4 Carefully lift the pancakes out of the pan, drain on kitchen paper and keep warm while you cook the remaining mixture in the same way. Sprinkle the pancakes with grated Parmesan cheese and serve with the salsa.

NUTRITION NOTES

Per portion:	
Energy	109Kcal/456kJ
Protein	3.9g
Fat	8.7g
saturated fat	1.9g
Carbohydrate	3g
Fibre	0.93g
Calcium	70.8mg

sautéed mussels with garlic and herbs

SHELLFISH IS ALWAYS a healthy choice as it is rich in valuable nutrients such as B vitamins, zinc, iron and selenium, which are essential for good health. Mussels are a good source of protein and are low in fat and carbohydrate.

4 Pull the mussels apart and carefully remove the flesh from the shells. Pat the mussels dry on kitchen paper.

5 Heat the olive oil in a frying pan, add the mussels, and cook, stirring, for 1 minute. Remove from the pan with a slotted spoon and set aside. Add the shallots and garlic to the pan and cook, covered, over a low heat for about 5 minutes, until soft and translucent, but not browned.

6 Remove the pan from the heat and stir in the chopped parsley, paprika and chilli. Return to the heat and stir in the mussels. Cook briefly. Remove from the heat and set aside, covered, for about 2 minutes before serving.

Serves 4

900g/2lb live mussels
1 lemon slice
45ml/3 tbsp olive oil
2 shallots, finely chopped
1 garlic clove, finely chopped
15ml/1 tbsp chopped fresh parsley
2.5ml/½ tsp paprika
1.5ml/¼ tsp dried chilli flakes

COOK'S TIP

Mussels are best cooked and eaten on the day of purchase. However, you can keep them in a large container of lightly salted water for a day.

1 Scrub the mussels and scrape off the beard. Discard any damaged specimens or any that do not close when tapped with the back of a knife.

2 Put the remaining mussels in a large pan, with 250ml/8fl oz/1 cup water and the lemon slice. Bring to the boil, cover tightly and cook over a high heat, shaking the pan occasionally, for about 4 minutes.

3 Remove the open mussels from the pan with a slotted spoon. Return the remaining mussels to the heat and cook for 1–2 minutes more. Remove any that open and discard those that remain closed.

NUTRITION NOTES

Per portion:	
Energy	241Kcal/1007kJ
Protein	27g
Fat	12.3g
saturated fat	2g
Carbohydrate	5.8g
Fibre	0.09g
Calcium	87mg

garlic prawns

THIS WONDERFUL, BUT SIMPLE dish with its aroma of garlic and hint of chilli only takes minutes to cook, so it is perfect for entertaining. Serve it for a dinner party, and your guests will never guess that you are following a diet.

rves 4
50–450g/12oz–1lb raw prawns (shrimp)
fresh red chillies
5ml/3 tbsp olive oil
garlic cloves, crushed
lt and ground black pepper

Remove the heads and shells from the prawns, leaving the tails intact. Remove the ark vein along the back of the prawns with sharp knife or a pin.

Halve each chilli lengthways and discard the seeds. Heat the oil in a ameproof pan, suitable for serving.

Add the prawns, chillies and garlic to the pan and cook over a high heat for minutes, stirring constantly until the prawns urn pink. Season and serve immediately.

VARIATIONS
• To add extra spice, stir 10ml/2 tsp finely chopped fresh root ginger into the pan with the chillies and garlic.
• To make a light lunch, serve the prawns on a bed of colourful mixed salad leaves and fresh herbs, such as coriander (cilantro) or mint.
• For a special occasion, use lobster tails or crawfish instead of prawns.

NUTRITION NOTES

Per portion:
Energy	226Kcal/944kJ
Protein	35g
Fat	9.4g
saturated fat	1.4g
Carbohydrate	0g
Fibre	0g
Calcium	43.6mg

ceviche with avocado salsa

THIS SIMPLE, NUTRITIOUS South American dish of marinated fish makes a delicious appetizer. Fish is a good low-fat source of protein, while olive oil and avocado provide healthy mono-unsaturated fats.

Serves 6

675g/1½lb halibut, sea bass or salmon
  fillets, skinned
juice of 3 limes
1–2 fresh red chillies, seeded and very
  finely chopped
15ml/1 tbsp olive oil
30ml/2 tbsp fresh coriander
  (cilantro) leaves
salt

For the salsa

1 ripe avocado
4 large firm tomatoes, peeled, seeded
  and diced
15ml/1 tbsp lemon juice
30ml/2 tbsp olive oil

1 Cut the fish into strips measuring about 5 x 1cm/2 x ½in. Lay these in a shallow, non-metallic dish and pour over the lime juice, turning the fish strips to coat them well. Cover and leave to stand for 1 hour.

2 Meanwhile, make the salsa. Cut the avocado in half and scoop out the stone (pit) with the point of a knife. Peel and dice the flesh. Place in a bowl and add the tomatoes, lemon juice and olive oil and mix well. Cover with clear film (plastic wrap) and set aside in a cool place until required.

3 Season the fish with salt and sprinkle over the chillies. Drizzle with the olive oil. Toss the fish in the mixture, then replace the cover. Leave to marinate in the refrigerator for about 25 minutes more.

4 To serve, divide the salsa among six individual serving plates. Spoon on the ceviche, sprinkle with coriander leaves and serve immediately.

NUTRITION NOTES

Per portion:

Energy	234Kcal/978kJ
Protein	25.3g
Fat	13.2g
saturated fat	2.5g
Carbohydrate	3.8g
Fibre	1.9g
Calcium	43.6mg

seafood salad

CRISP SALAD LEAVES and fresh shellfish are a tasty combination that fit perfectly within a diet because both are naturally low in carbohydrate. You can vary the choice of seafood according to what is available.

Serves 6

450g/1lb live mussels, scrubbed
  and bearded
450g/1lb small clams, scrubbed
105ml/7 tbsp dry white wine
225g/8oz squid, cleaned
4 large scallops, with their corals
30ml/2 tbsp olive oil
2 garlic cloves, finely chopped
1 small dried red chilli, crumbled
225g/8oz cooked unpeeled
  prawns (shrimp)
6–8 large chicory (Belgian endive) leaves
6–8 radicchio leaves
15ml/1 tbsp chopped flat leaf parsley,
  to garnish

For the dressing

5ml/1 tsp Dijon mustard
30ml/2 tbsp white wine or cider vinegar
5ml/1 tsp lemon juice
75ml/5 tbsp extra virgin olive oil
salt and ground black pepper

1 Put the mussels and clams in a large pan and pour in the white wine. Cover tightly and cook over a high heat, shaking the pan occasionally, for about 4 minutes, until the shells have opened. Discard any that remain closed. Use a slotted spoon to transfer the shellfish to a bowl, then strain and reserve the cooking liquid.

2 Cut the squid bodies into thin rings and chop the tentacles into bitesize pieces. Leave any small squid whole. Halve the scallops horizontally.

3 Heat the olive oil in a frying pan, add the garlic, chilli, squid, scallops and their corals, and sauté over a low heat for about 2 minutes, until just cooked and tender. Lift the squid, scallops and corals out of the pan. Reserve the oil.

4 When the mussels and clams are cool, shell them, keeping 12 of each in the shell. Peel all but six of the prawns.

5 Strain the shellfish cooking liquid into a small pan, set over a high heat, bring to the boil and reduce by half. In a large bowl, combine all the mussels and clams with the squid and scallops, then add the prawns.

6 To make the dressing, whisk the mustard with the wine or vinegar and lemon juice and season. Add the olive oil, whisk, then whisk in the reduced cooking liquid and oil from the frying pan. Pour the dressing over the seafood mixture and toss lightly.

7 Arrange the salad leaves around the edge of a large serving dish and pile the seafood mixture into the centre. Sprinkle with the parsley and serve immediately.

NUTRITION NOTES

Per portion:	
Energy	252Kcal/1053kJ
Protein	26.5g
Fat	13.5g
saturated fat	2.2g
Carbohydrate	3.9g
Fibre	0.07g
Calcium	106mg

main meal
salads

GENEROUS, LEAFY GREEN SALADS can easily be turned into a nutritious main meal with the addition of ingredients such as fish, poultry or meat. They are healthy and satisfying, offering essential fibre, nutrients and sustaining low-fat protein, which makes them perfect for a low-carbohydrate diet. All the recipes in this chapter are simple to prepare, taste delicious and fit easily into your weekly menu and healthy eating plan.

greek salad

THIS WONDERFULLY TANGY SALAD makes a perfect lunch or supper dish. The combination of tomatoes, cucumber, lettuce olives, cheese and lemon juice offers a range of nutrients from vitamins C and E to monounsaturated fats and protein.

Serves 4

1 small cos or romaine
  lettuce, sliced
450g/1lb well-flavoured tomatoes,
  cut into eighths
1 cucumber, seeded and chopped
200g/7oz feta cheese, crumbled
4 spring onions (scallions), sliced
50g/2oz/½ cup black olives, pitted
  and halved

For the dressing

45ml/3 tbsp olive oil
25ml/1½ tbsp lemon juice
salt and ground black pepper

NUTRITION NOTES

Per portion:	
Energy	240Kcal/1002kJ
Protein	9.5g
Fat	20.4g
saturated fat	8.4g
Carbohydrate	5.4g
Fibre	2.25g
Calcium	210mg

1 Put the lettuce, tomatoes, cucumber, crumbled feta cheese, spring onions and olives in a large salad bowl.

2 For the dressing, whisk together the olive oil and lemon juice, then seaso Pour over the salad, toss well and serve.

varm salad with poached eggs

SOFT POACHED EGGS, chilli oil, hot croûtons and cool, crisp salad leaves make a lively and unusual combination. This delicious salad will provide a sustaining lunch or supper.

ves 2

nl/1½ tbsp chilli oil
ice wholegrain bread, crusts removed
nd cubed
ggs
5g/4oz mixed salad leaves
nl/3 tbsp extra virgin olive oil
arlic cloves, crushed
nl/1 tbsp balsamic or
herry vinegar
g/2oz Parmesan
heese, shaved
und black pepper (optional)

leat the chilli oil in a large frying pan. Add
ne cubes of bread and cook for 5 minutes,
ing the cubes occasionally, until they are
o and golden brown all over. Remove the
utons from the pan and place them on
hen paper to drain off any excess oil.

Bring a pan of water to a gentle boil.
Break each egg into a jug (pitcher) and
e into the water. Poach for 3–4 minutes.
anwhile, divide the salad leaves
ween two plates.

Remove the croûtons from the pan and
scatter them over the salad leaves.
pe the pan clean, then add the olive oil
l heat. Add the garlic and vinegar and
k over a high heat for 1 minute. Pour
warm dressing over the salads.

4 Pat the poached eggs dry on kitchen
paper, then carefully place one egg
on top of each salad.

5 Top each salad with thin Parmesan
shavings and a little freshly ground
black pepper, if using.

NUTRITION NOTES

Per portion:	
Energy	447Kcal/1868kJ
Protein	20.7g
Fat	33.6g
saturated fat	9.7g
Carbohydrate	8.5g
Fibre	1.6g
Calcium	361mg

salad with omelette strips and bacon

CRISP BACON AND HERBY OMELETTE STRIPS add substanc
and protein to this light and tasty salad.

Serves 4

6 streaky (fatty) bacon rashers
(strips), rinds removed
and chopped
400g/14oz mixed salad leaves,
including some distinctively flavoured
leaves such as rocket (arugula),
watercress and fresh herbs
2 eggs
2 spring onions (scallions), chopped
few sprigs of coriander
(cilantro), chopped
25g/1oz/2 tbsp butter
60ml/4 tbsp olive oil
30ml/2 tbsp balsamic vinegar
salt and ground black pepper

1 Warm an omelette pan over a low heat.
Add the chopped bacon and cook gently
until the fat runs. Increase the heat to crisp the
bacon, stirring frequently. When the bacon
pieces are brown and crispy, remove from the
heat and transfer to a hot dish to keep warm.

2 Place the salad leaves in a large bowl.
In another bowl, beat the eggs with
the chopped spring onions and coriander
and season well with salt and pepper.

3 Melt the butter in the omelette pan
and pour in the eggs. Cook for about
3 minutes to make an unfolded omelette.
Cut into long strips and keep warm.

4 Add the oil, vinegar and seasoning
the pan and heat briefly. Sprinkle th
bacon and omelette strips over the salad
leaves, then pour over the dressing. Toss

NUTRITION NOTES

Per portion:

Energy	321Kcal/1341
Protein	13.4
Fat	28.9
saturated fat	9.0
Carbohydrate	2.2
Fibre	0.9
Calcium	49.2m

chilli salad omelettes with hummus

THESE DELICATE OMELETTES filled with healthy and nutritious
salad make a refreshing low-carbohydrate lunch.

Serves 4

4 eggs
15ml/1 tbsp cornflour (cornstarch)
115g/4oz/1 cup shredded salad
vegetables
60ml/4 tbsp chilli salad dressing
60–75ml/4–5 tbsp hummus
4 cooked bacon rashers (strips), chopped
salt and ground black pepper

NUTRITION NOTES

Per portion:

Energy	358Kcal/1498kJ
Protein	19.05g
Fat	29.1g
saturated fat	6.75g
Carbohydrate	6.15g
Fibre	0.75g
Calcium	54mg

1 Beat together the eggs, cornflour and
15ml/1 tbsp water in a bowl. Heat a
lightly oiled frying pan and pour a quarter
of the mixture into the pan, tipping it to
spread it out to a thin, even layer. Cook
the omelette gently. When cooked, remove
from the pan and make 3 more omelettes in
the same way. Stack them between sheets
of baking parchment, then chill.

2 When ready to serve, toss the
shredded salad vegetables together
with about 45ml/3 tbsp of the dressing.

3 Spread half of each omelette with
hummus, top with the salad vegetab
and chopped bacon and fold in half.
Drizzle the rest of the dressing over the
filled omelettes before serving.

warm monkfish salad

GRIDDLED MONKFISH tossed with nutritious pine nuts and vitamin-rich baby spinach is a delicious combination that will make you forget you are on a diet.

Serves 4

2 monkfish fillets, each weighing about
  350g/12oz
25g/1oz/¼ cup pine nuts
15ml/1 tbsp olive oil
225g/8oz baby spinach leaves, washed
  and stalks removed
salt and ground black pepper

For the dressing
5ml/1 tsp Dijon mustard
5ml/1 tsp sherry vinegar
30ml/2 tbsp olive oil
1 garlic clove, crushed

VARIATION
Substitute salad leaves for the spinach if you like. Watercress and rocket (arugula) would be good alternatives.

1 Holding the knife at a slight angle, cut each monkfish fillet into 12 diagonal slices. Season lightly and set aside.

2 Heat a dry frying pan, put in the pine nuts and shake them over a low heat, until golden brown but not burned. Transfer to a plate and set aside.

3 To make the dressing, put the mustard, sherry vinegar, olive oil and garlic in a jug (pitcher) or small bowl and whisk thoroughly until smooth and creamy. Pour the dressing into a small pan, season to taste with salt and pepper and warm through over a low heat.

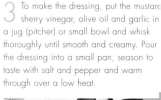

4 Heat the oil in a ridged griddle pan frying pan until sizzling. Add the fish slices and sauté for about 20–30 seconds on each side.

5 Put the spinach leaves into a large bowl and pour over the warm salad dressing. Sprinkle on the toasted pine nuts, reserving a few, and toss together well. Divide the dressed spinach leaves among four serving plates and arrange the fish slices on top. Sprinkle over the reserved pine nuts and serve immediately.

NUTRITION NOTES

Per portion:	
Energy	222Kcal/927kJ
Protein	29.9g
Fat	10.9g
saturated fat	1.3g
Carbohydrate	1.1g
Fibre	1.3g
Calcium	110.3mg

warm swordfish and peppery salad

ROBUST SWORDFISH teamed with peppery salad makes a
healthy meal that's perfect for any occasion, whether it's part
of a low-carbohydrate eating plan or a sophisticated dinner.

rves **4**

swordfish steaks
ml/5 tbsp extra virgin olive oil
ce of 1 lemon
ml/2 tbsp finely chopped
fresh parsley
5g/4oz rocket (arugula) leaves
5g/4oz Pecorino cheese
t and ground black pepper

1 Lay the swordfish steaks in a shallow
dish. In a small jug (pitcher) or bowl, mix
about 60ml/4 tbsp of the olive oil with the
lemon juice. Pour the mixture over the fish.
Season with salt and ground black pepper,
sprinkle on the finely chopped parsley and
turn the fish to coat well. Cover with clear
film (plastic wrap) and leave to marinate for
at least 10 minutes.

2 Heat a ridged griddle pan or the grill
(broiler) until very hot. Remove the fish
steaks from the marinade and pat dry with
kitchen paper.

3 Place the fish steaks in the griddle pan
or under the grill (broiler) and cook for
2 minutes on each side until the swordfish
is opaque and just cooked through.

4 Meanwhile, remove the stems from the
rocket leaves and put the leaves in a
large bowl. Season with salt and pepper.
Drizzle over the remaining olive oil and
toss well to combine. Shave the Pecorino
cheese over the top of the salad leaves.

5 Place the swordfish steaks on four
individual plates and arrange a little
pile of salad on each steak. Serve
immediately, while still warm.

NUTRITION NOTES

Per portion:	
Energy	451Kcal/1885kJ
Protein	43.6g
Fat	30.5g
saturated fat	9.5g
Carbohydrate	0.5g
Fibre	0.6g
Calcium	400mg

salad niçoise

THIS CLASSIC FRENCH SALAD makes a simple yet unbeatable meal. It offers the perfect combination of low-carbohydrate salad vegetables and healthy oily fish.

Serves 4

115g/4oz green beans, trimmed
  and halved
115g/4oz mixed salad leaves
½ small cucumber, thinly sliced
4 ripe tomatoes, quartered
1 tuna steak, weighing about 175g/6oz
olive oil, for brushing
50g/2oz can anchovies, drained and
  halved lengthways
4 eggs, hard-boiled, shelled and quartered
½ bunch small radishes, trimmed
50g/2oz/½ cup small black olives
salt and ground black pepper

For the dressing

90ml/6 tbsp extra virgin olive oil
2 garlic cloves, crushed
15ml/1 tbsp white wine vinegar

1 To make the dressing, whisk all the ingredients together and season to taste.

2 Cook the beans in boiling water for 2 minutes, until just tender, then drain. In a large shallow bowl, combine the salad leaves, sliced cucumber, tomatoes and beans.

3 Preheat the grill (broiler). Brush the tuna with olive oil and season. Grill (broil) for 3–4 minutes on each side until cooked through. Leave to cool, then flake.

4 Sprinkle the flaked tuna, anchovies, quartered eggs, radishes and olives over the salad. Pour over the dressing and toss lightly to combine, then serve.

NUTRITION NOTES

Per portion:	
Energy	355Kcal/1483kJ
Protein	21.4g
Fat	28.3g
saturated fat	4.8g
Carbohydrate	4.2g
Fibre	2.3g
Calcium	109mg

crab salad with capers

COMBINING TANGY CITRUS JUICE, sweet peppers and crab offers a powerhouse of valuable nutrients including vitamin C, B vitamins, zinc, potassium and betacarotene.

Serves 4

white and brown meat from 4 small
  fresh dressed crabs, about
  450g/1lb
small red (bell) pepper, seeded
  and finely chopped
small red onion, finely chopped
30ml/2 tbsp drained capers
30ml/2 tbsp chopped fresh
  coriander (cilantro)
grated rind and juice of 2 lemons
Tabasco sauce
40g/1½oz rocket (arugula) leaves
30ml/2 tbsp sunflower oil
15ml/1 tbsp fresh lime juice
salt and ground black pepper
lemon rind strips, to garnish

1 Put the crab meat, red pepper, onion, capers and coriander in a bowl. Add the lemon rind and juice and toss gently to mix. Season to taste with Tabasco sauce, salt and ground black pepper.

2 Wash the rocket leaves and pat dry. Divide among four plates. Mix the oil and lime juice in a small bowl. Dress the leaves, then pile the crab salad on top and serve garnished with strips of lemon rind.

NUTRITION NOTES

Per portion:	
Energy	156Kcal/652kJ
Protein	21.3g
Fat	6.3g
saturated fat	0.8g
Carbohydrate	3.9g
Fibre	1.1g
Calcium	159mg

citrus chicken salad

THIS ATTRACTIVE, ZESTY SALAD offers a delicious combinatic of healthy raw vegetables, lean, grilled chicken and oranges and limes, which are rich in vitamin C.

Serves 6

6 skinless boneless chicken
   breast portions
4 oranges
5ml/1 tsp Dijon mustard
15ml/3 tsp clear honey
60ml/4 tbsp extra virgin olive oil
300g/11oz/2¾ cups finely shredded
   white cabbage
300g/11oz carrots, peeled and
   thinly sliced
2 spring onions (scallions), thinly sliced
2 celery sticks, cut into thin batons
30ml/2 tbsp chopped fresh tarragon
2 limes
salt and ground black pepper

1 Place the chicken under a preheated grill (broiler) and cook for 5 minutes on each side, or until it is cooked through and golden brown. Leave to cool.

2 Peel two of the oranges, cutting off all pith, then cut out the segments and set aside. Grate the rind and squeeze the juice from one of the remaining oranges and place in a bowl.

3 Stir the mustard, 5ml/1 tsp of the honey, the oil and seasoning into the orange juice. Mix in the cabbage, carrots, spring onions and celery, then leave to stand for 10 minutes.

4 Meanwhile, squeeze the juice from the remaining orange and mix it with the remaining honey and tarragon. Peel and segment the limes and lightly mix the segments into the dressing with the reserved orange segments and seasoning to taste.

5 Slice the chicken and stir into the dressing with the oranges and limes. Divide the vegetables among six plates, add the chicken, then serve.

NUTRITION NOTES

Per portion:	
Energy	303Kcal/1226kJ
Protein	48.8g
Fat	10.7g
saturated fat	1.9g
Carbohydrate	2.8g
Fibre	1.2g
Calcium	39.5mg

spiced quail and mushroom salad

A WARM SALAD of grilled quail, walnuts, mushrooms and salad leaves is perfect for a hearty autumn or winter meal. It is warming and tasty yet contains barely any carbohydrate.

erves 4
quail breasts
ml/1 tsp paprika
lt and ground black pepper

or the salad
5g/1oz/2 tbsp butter
5g/3oz/generous 1 cup chanterelle mushrooms, sliced if large
5g/1oz/3 tbsp walnut halves, toasted
0ml/2 tbsp walnut oil
0ml/2 tbsp olive oil
5ml/3 tbsp balsamic vinegar
15g/4oz mixed salad leaves

Preheat the grill (broiler). Arrange the quail breasts on the grill rack, skin-sides p. Sprinkle with half the paprika and a tle salt.

2 Grill (broil) the breasts for 3 minutes, then turn them over and sprinkle with the emaining paprika and a little salt. Grill for further 3 minutes, or until cooked through. ransfer the quail breasts to a warmed dish, over with foil and leave to stand while reparing the salad.

3 Heat the butter in a frying pan until foaming and cook the chanterelles for bout 3 minutes, or until just beginning to often. Add the walnuts and heat through. emove from the heat.

4 Meanwhile, make the dressing, whisk the oils with the balsamic vinegar, then season and set aside.

5 Using a sharp knife, slice the cooked quail breasts thinly and arrange them on four individual serving plates with the warmed chanterelle mushrooms and walnuts and mixed salad leaves. Drizzle the oil and vinegar dressing over the salad and serve immediately while still warm.

NUTRITION NOTES

Per portion:	
Energy	353Kcal/1391kJ
Protein	42.9g
Fat	19.8g
saturated fat	5.7g
Carbohydrate	0.7g
Fibre	0.6g
Calcium	22.6mg

warm duck salad with poached eggs

GRILLED DUCK SKEWERS look and taste wonderful in this spectacular salad. It makes the ideal choice for a special meal that won't run the risk of ruining your healthy eating plan.

4 Meanwhile, heat the groundnut oil in a frying pan and cook the chopped shallot until softened. Add the mushrooms and cook over a high heat for 5 minutes, stirring occasionally.

5 While the chanterelles are cooking, half fill a frying pan with water, add a little salt and heat until simmering. Break the eggs one at a time into a cup, then gently tip into the water. Poach the eggs gently for about 3 minutes, or until the whites are set. Use a slotted spoon to transfer the eggs to a warm plate, pat dry with kitchen paper, then trim off any untidy white.

6 Arrange the salad leaves on four plates, then add the chanterelles and skewered duck. Place the eggs on the salad. Drizzle with olive oil and season with pepper, then serve immediately.

Serves 4

3 skinless, boneless duck breasts,
  thinly sliced
30ml/2 tbsp soy sauce
30ml/2 tbsp balsamic vinegar
30ml/2 tbsp groundnut (peanut) oil
1 shallot, finely chopped
115g/4oz/1½ cups chanterelle mushrooms
4 eggs
50g/2oz mixed salad leaves
salt and ground black pepper
30ml/2 tbsp extra virgin olive oil,
  to serve

1 Put the duck in a shallow dish and toss with the soy sauce and balsamic vinegar. Cover and chill for 30 minutes. Meanwhile, soak 12 bamboo skewers (about 13cm/5in long) in water to help prevent them from burning during cooking.

2 Preheat the grill (broiler). Thread the marinated duck slices on to the skewers, pleating them neatly.

3 Place the skewers on a grill pan and cook for 3–5 minutes, then turn the skewers and cook for a further 3 minutes, or until the duck is golden brown.

NUTRITION NOTES

Per portion:	
Energy	321Kcal/1341kJ
Protein	36.5g
Fat	19.4g
saturated fat	3.9g
Carbohydrate	0.2g
Fibre	0.09g
Calcium	45.1mg

hai beef salad

THIS QUICK AND HEALTHY traditional Thai dish provides a good source of vitamin C, folic acid, iron, potassium, zinc and the health-giving phytochemical lycopene.

erves 6

75g/1½lb fillet or rump (round) steak

ml/2 tbsp olive oil

small mild red chillies, seeded
and sliced

25g/8oz/3¼ cups shiitake
mushrooms, sliced

r the dressing

spring onions (scallions), finely chopped

garlic cloves, finely chopped

ice of 1 lime

5–30ml/1–2 tbsp Thai fish sauce or
oyster sauce, to taste

ml/2 tbsp chopped fresh coriander
(cilantro)

 serve

cos or romaine lettuce, torn into strips

75g/6oz cherry tomatoes, halved

cm/2in piece cucumber, peeled, halved
and thinly sliced

5ml/3 tbsp toasted sesame seeds

NUTRITION NOTES

Per portion:

Energy	332Kcal/1387kJ
Protein	40.4g
Fat	18.2g
saturated fat	4.5g
Carbohydrate	2.1g
Fibre	1.6g
Calcium	105.8mg

Preheat the grill (broiler) until hot, then cook the steak for 2–4 minutes on each de depending on how well done you like our steak. Leave to stand and firm up for t least 15 minutes.

2 Use a very sharp knife to slice the meat as thinly as possible and place he slices in a bowl.

3 Heat the olive oil in a small frying pan. Add the red chillies and mushrooms and cook for 5 minutes, stirring occasionally. Turn off the heat and add the grilled steak slices to the pan, then stir well to coat the beef slices in the chilli and mushroom mixture.

4 Stir all the ingredients for the dressing together, then pour it over the meat mixture and toss gently. Arrange the salad ingredients on a serving plate. Spoon the steak mixture in the centre and sprinkle the sesame seeds over. Serve immediately.

hot
main meals

HOT MEALS ARE A MAIN PART of most people's weekly menu, but they don't have to be a danger zone of high-carbohydrate, comfort food. Whatever your taste, from hot and spicy to subtle and delicate, there is a perfect low-carbohydrate main meal option. For optimum nutrition, always serve these dishes with a large mixed leaf salad or a low-carbohydrate vegetable dish.

creamy lemon puy lentils

WHOLESOME LENTILS provide slowly-absorbed carbohydrate that provide energy but avoid an exaggerated insulin response which can be caused by quickly-absorbed carbohydrates.

Serves 6

250g/9oz/generous 1 cup Puy lentils
1 bay leaf
30ml/2 tbsp olive oil
4 spring onions (scallions), sliced
2 large garlic cloves, chopped
15ml/1 tbsp Dijon mustard
finely grated rind and juice of
    1 large lemon
4 plum tomatoes, seeded and diced
6 eggs
60ml/4 tbsp crème fraîche
salt and ground black pepper
30ml/2 tbsp chopped fresh flat leaf
    parsley, to garnish

1 Put the lentils and bay leaf in a pan, cover with cold water, and bring to the boil. Reduce the heat and simmer, partially covered, for 25 minutes, or until the lentils are tender. Stir the lentils occasionally and add more water, if necessary. Drain.

2 Heat the oil in a frying pan and cook the spring onions and garlic for about 1 minute or until softened. Add the Dijon mustard, lemon rind and juice, and mix.

3 Stir the tomatoes and seasoning into the onion mixture, then cook gently for 1–2 minutes until the tomatoes are heated through, but still retain their shape. Add a little water if the mixture becomes too dry.

4 Meanwhile, poach the eggs in a pan of lightly salted barely simmering water for 4 minutes, adding them one at a time.

5 Gently stir the lentils and crème fraîche into the tomato mixture, remove and discard the bay leaf, and heat through for 1 minute. Divide the mixture among six serving plates. Top each portion with a poached egg, and sprinkle with parsley. Serve immediately.

NUTRITION NOTES

Per portion:	
Energy	232Kcal/969kJ
Protein	14.9g
Fat	10.2g
saturated fat	2.9g
Carbohydrate	21.7g
Fibre	4.1g
Calcium	62.3mg

frittata with sun-dried tomatoes

THIS ITALIAN OMELETTE can be served warm or cold. Enjoy it with a large leafy green salad or a generous serving of low-carbohydrate vegetables such as spinach or broccoli.

Serves 4

sun-dried tomatoes
0ml/4 tbsp olive oil
small onion, finely chopped
inch of fresh thyme leaves
eggs
5g/1oz/⅓ cup freshly grated Parmesan
cheese, plus shavings to serve
alt and ground black pepper
yme sprigs, to garnish

Place the tomatoes in a bowl and pour over hot water to cover. Leave to soak for 5 minutes. Lift out the tomatoes and pat ry on kitchen paper. Reserve the soaking ater. Cut the tomatoes into thin strips.

2 Heat the olive oil in a frying pan. Cook the onion for 5–6 minutes. Add ne thyme and tomatoes and cook for a urther 2–3 minutes.

3 Break the eggs into a bowl and beat lightly. Stir in 45ml/3 tbsp of the tomato soaking water and the Parmesan and season to taste. Raise the heat under the pan. When the oil is sizzling, add the eggs. Mix quickly into the other ingredients, then stop stirring. Lower the heat to medium and cook for 4–5 minutes, or until the base is golden and the top puffed.

4 Take a large plate, invert it over the pan and, holding it firmly with oven gloves, turn the pan and the frittata over on to it. Slide the frittata back into the pan, and continue cooking for 3–4 minutes until golden brown on the second side. Remove the pan from the heat. Cut the frittata into wedges, garnish with thyme sprigs and serve immediately or leave to cool.

NUTRITION NOTES

Per portion:

Energy	335Kcal/1400kJ
Protein	12.6g
Fat	30.8g
saturated fat	6.4g
Carbohydrate	2.2g
Fibre	0.2g
Calcium	127mg

steamed lettuce-wrapped sole

COOKING FOOD IN STEAM is extremely healthy as it helps t
retain the nutrients that can be lost by other cooking methods. I
also gives wonderfully succulent results.

Serves 4

2 large sole fillets, skinned
15ml/1 tbsp sesame seeds
15ml/1 tbsp sunflower or groundnut
   (peanut) oil
2.5cm/1in piece fresh root ginger,
   peeled and grated
3 garlic cloves, finely chopped
15ml/1 tbsp soy sauce or
   Thai fish sauce
juice of 1 lemon
2 spring onions (scallions),
   thinly sliced
8 large soft lettuce leaves
12 large live mussels, scrubbed
   and bearded
salt and ground black pepper
sesame oil, for drizzling (optional)

1 Cut the sole fillets in half lengthways.
Season with salt and ground black
pepper, then set aside.

2 Heat a heavy frying pan until hot.
Toast the sesame seeds lightly, being
careful not to let them burn, then set aside.

3 Heat the sunflower or groundnut oil in
the frying pan. Add the ginger and
garlic and cook, stirring, until lightly
coloured but not browned; stir in the soy
sauce or Thai fish sauce, lemon juice and
spring onions. Remove the pan from the
heat and stir in the toasted sesame seeds.

4 Lay the pieces of fish on baking
parchment, skinned side up; spread
each evenly with the ginger mixture. Roll
up each piece, starting at the tail end and
place the rolls on a baking sheet.

5 Bring a pan of water, over which the
steamer will fit, to the boil. Plunge the
lettuce leaves into the boiling water and
immediately lift them out. Lay them out flat
on kitchen paper and pat dry.

6 Tightly wrap each sole parcel in two
lettuce leaves, making sure they are
very secure. Arrange the fish parcels in the
steamer basket, cover and steam over
simmering water for 8 minutes.

7 Add the mussels to the steamer and
steam for 2–4 minutes, until they open
Discard any that remain closed. Put the
parcels on four plates and garnish with the
mussels. Serve drizzled with oil, if liked.

NUTRITION NOTES

Per portion:	
Energy	136Kcal/568kJ
Protein	17.4g
Fat	7.1g
saturated fat	1.0g
Carbohydrate	0.6g
Fibre	0.3g
Calcium	46.5mg

chinese-style steamed trout

TROUT IS RICH IN ESSENTIAL fatty acids, which are vital for good health. Serve this dish with a low-carbohydrate vegetable dish such as stir-fried spring greens.

Serves 6

trout, each weighing about
675–800g/1½–1¾lb
5ml/1½ tbsp salted black beans
5ml/½ tsp sugar
0ml/2 tbsp finely shredded fresh
root ginger
garlic cloves, thinly sliced
0ml/2 tbsp Chinese rice wine or
dry sherry
0ml/2 tbsp light soy sauce
–6 spring onions (scallions), finely
shredded or sliced diagonally
5ml/3 tbsp groundnut
(peanut) oil
0ml/2 tsp sesame oil

1 Wash the fish inside and out under cold running water, then pat dry on kitchen paper. Using a sharp knife, slash 3–4 deep crosses on each side of each fish.

2 Place half the black beans and the sugar in a small bowl and mash together with the back of a fork. Stir in the remaining whole beans.

3 Place a little ginger and garlic inside the cavity of each fish, then lay them on a plate or dish that will fit inside a large steamer. Rub the bean mixture into the fish, working it into the slashes, then sprinkle the remaining ginger and garlic over the top. Cover with clear film (plastic wrap) and place the fish in the refrigerator for at least 0 minutes.

4 Remove the fish from the refrigerator and place the steamer over a pan of boiling water. Sprinkle the rice wine or sherry and half the soy sauce over the fish and place the plate of fish inside the steamer. Steam for 15–20 minutes, or until the fish is just cooked and the flesh flakes easily when tested with a fork.

5 Using a fish slice (metal spatula), carefully lift the fish on to a warmed serving dish. Sprinkle the fish with the remaining soy sauce and then sprinkle with the shredded or sliced spring onions.

6 In a small pan, heat the groundnut oil until very hot and smoking, then trickle it over the spring onions and fish. Lightly sprinkle the sesame oil over the fish and serve immediately.

NUTRITION NOTES

Per portion:

Energy	378Kcal/1580kJ
Protein	52.4g
Fat	18.7g
saturated fat	3.5g
Carbohydrate	0.2g
Fibre	0.1g
Calcium	50.6mg

salmon with leeks and peppers

ATTRACTIVE PAPER PARCELS OF FISH are as healthy as they ar
tasty. The fish and vegetables cook in their own juices, allowing
them to retain all their valuable nutrients.

4 When the vegetable mixture is cool,
divide it equally among the rounds
and top with a portion of salmon.

5 Drizzle each portion of fish with a lit
sesame oil and sprinkle with the
remaining chives and the chopped fennel
fronds. Season with a little more salt and
ground black pepper.

6 Fold the baking parchment or foil ove
to enclose the fish, rolling and twistin
the edges together to seal the parcels.

7 Place the parcels on a baking sheet
and bake for 15–20 minutes, or unti
the parcels are puffed up and, if made
with parchment, lightly browned. Carefull
transfer the parcels to six warmed plates
and serve immediately, still wrapped in
baking parchment or foil.

Serves 6

25ml/1½ tbsp groundnut (peanut) oil
2 yellow (bell) peppers, seeded and
thinly sliced
4cm/1½in fresh root ginger, peeled and
finely shredded
1 large fennel bulb, thinly sliced, fronds
chopped and reserved
1 fresh green chilli, seeded and
finely shredded
2 large leeks, cut into 10cm/4in lengths
and shredded lengthways
30ml/2 tbsp chopped fresh chives
10ml/2 tsp light soy sauce
6 portions salmon fillet, each weighing
about 150–175g/5–6oz, skinned
10ml/2 tsp toasted sesame oil
salt and ground black pepper

1 Heat the oil in a large non-stick frying
pan. Add the yellow peppers, ginger and
fennel bulb and cook, stirring occasionally,
for 5–6 minutes, until they are softened,
but not browned.

2 Add the fresh green chilli and leeks to
the pan and cook, stirring occasionally,
for about 3 minutes. Stir in half the chopped
chives and the soy sauce and season to taste
with a little salt and freshly ground black
pepper. Set the vegetable mixture aside to
cool slightly.

3 Meanwhile, preheat the oven to
190°C/375°F/Gas 5. Cut six 35cm/
14in rounds of baking parchment or foil
and set aside.

NUTRITION NOTES

Per portion:

Energy	325Kcal/1358k]
Protein	31.6g
Fat	20.5g
saturated fat	3.4g
Carbohydrate	4.0g
Fibre	2.1g
Calcium	48.2mg

grilled sea bass with fennel

THIS IS AN IMPRESSIVE DISH that is perfect for entertaining. Serve it to guests, and they will never guess that this opulent dish could be part of a healthy-eating, weight loss diet.

Serves 8

1 sea bass, weighing 1.8–2kg/4–4½lb
60ml/4 tbsp olive oil
10–15ml/2–3 tsp fennel seeds
2 large fennel bulbs, trimmed and thinly
  sliced (reserve any fronds)
60ml/4 tbsp Pernod
salt and ground black pepper

NUTRITION NOTES

Per portion:

Energy	308Kcal/1287kJ
Protein	37.1g
Fat	15.3g
saturated fat	2.9g
Carbohydrate	3.2g
Fibre	0.9g
Calcium	43.7mg

1 With a sharp knife, make 3–4 deep cuts in both sides of the fish. Brush the fish with olive oil and season with salt and plenty of ground black pepper.

2 Sprinkle the fennel seeds in the cavity and into the cuts on both sides of the fish. Set aside while you cook the fennel.

3 Preheat the grill (broiler). Put the slices of fennel in a flameproof dish or on the grill rack and brush with a little olive oil. Cook for 4 minutes on each side until just tender. Transfer the fennel to a serving plate and set aside while you grill (broil) the fish.

4 Place the fish on the grill rack and position about 10–14cm/4–5½in away from the heat. Grill for 12 minutes on each side, brushing with oil occasionally during cooking.

5 Transfer the fish to the serving platter, placing it on top of the grilled fennel. Sprinkle over any reserved fennel fronds.

6 Heat the Pernod in a small pan, ignite it and pour it, flaming, over the fish. Serve immediately.

seared tuna steaks with tomato salsa

FRESH AND FRUITY tomato salsa provides a delicious boost of vitamins to accompany the health-promoting omega-3 fatty acids that can be found in fresh tuna fish.

Serves 4

4 tuna steaks, each weighing about
    175–200g/6–7oz
30ml/2 tbsp extra virgin olive oil
5ml/1 tsp cumin seeds, toasted
grated rind and juice of 1 lime
pinch of dried red chilli flakes
1 small red onion, finely chopped
200g/7oz cherry tomatoes, chopped
1 avocado, peeled, stoned and chopped
2 kiwi fruit, peeled and chopped
1 fresh red chilli, seeded and chopped
15g/½oz fresh coriander
    (cilantro), chopped
6 fresh mint sprigs, leaves only, chopped
5–10ml/1–2 tsp Thai fish sauce
salt and ground black pepper
lime wedges and fresh coriander (cilantro)
    sprigs, to garnish

1 Place the tuna steaks on a glass or ceramic plate and drizzle over the extra virgin olive oil. Sprinkle the steaks with half the toasted cumin seeds, salt, ground black pepper, half the lime rind and the dried chilli flakes. Set aside and leave to stand for about 30 minutes.

2 Meanwhile, make the salsa. Combine the onion, tomatoes, avocado, kiwi fruit, chilli, coriander and mint in a bowl. Add the remaining cumin seeds and lime rind and half the lime juice. Stir in Thai fish sauce to taste. Cover with clear film (plastic wrap) and set aside for about 20 minutes, then taste and add more Thai fish sauce and lime juice, if necessary.

3 Heat a ridged, cast-iron griddle pan until very hot. Carefully lay the tuna steaks in the pan and cook for 2 minutes on each side for rare tuna or a little longer for a medium result.

4 Transfer the tuna steaks to four warmed serving plates and garnish with lime wedges and fresh coriander sprigs. Spoon on the tomato salsa, or transfer it to a serving bowl and offer it separately.

NUTRITION NOTES

Per portion:	
Energy	419Kcal/1751kJ
Protein	48.7g
Fat	22.9g
saturated fat	5.1g
Carbohydrate	4.9g
Fibre	2.3g
Calcium	49.4mg

chicken breasts with serrano ham

LEAN CHICKEN IS AN IDEAL CHOICE for anyone following a low-carbohydrate diet. For a well-balanced meal serve with a large mixed green leaf and herb salad.

Serves 4

4 skinless, boneless chicken
  breast portions
4 slices Serrano ham
40g/1½oz/3 tbsp butter
30ml/2 tbsp chopped capers
30ml/2 tbsp fresh thyme leaves
1 large lemon, cut lengthways
  into 8 slices
a few small fresh thyme sprigs
salt and ground black pepper

COOK'S TIP

This dish is just as good with other thinly sliced cured ham, such as prosciutto, in place of the Serrano ham.

1 Preheat the oven to 200°C/400°F/ Gas 6. Wrap each chicken breast portion loosely in clear film (plastic wrap) and beat with a rolling pin until flattened. Unwrap the chicken breast portions and arrange in a single layer in a large, shallow ovenproof dish. Top each piece of chicken with a slice of Serrano ham.

2 In a bowl, beat the butter with the capers, thyme and seasoning. Divide the butter into quarters and shape neat portions, then place on each ham-topped chicken breast portion. Arrange two lemon slices on the butter and sprinkle with thyme sprigs. Bake for 25 minutes, or until the chicken is cooked through.

3 Transfer the chicken portions to a warmed serving platter or four plates and spoon the piquant, buttery juices over the top. Serve immediately, removing the lemon slices first, if liked.

NUTRITION NOTES

Per portion:

Energy	352Kcal/1471kJ
Protein	52.7g
Fat	15.7g
saturated fat	8.5g
Carbohydrate	0g
Fibre	0g
Calcium	10.8mg

devilled chicken

GRILLING IS A VERY HEALTHY way of cooking meat, and these spicy chicken skewers are a good source of protein. Serve them with a crisp leaf salad for a nutritious main meal.

Serves 4
60ml/4 tbsp olive oil
finely grated rind and juice of 1 lemon
2 garlic cloves, finely chopped
10ml/2 tsp finely chopped or crumbled dried red chillies
12 skinless, boneless chicken thighs, each cut into 3 or 4 pieces
salt and ground black pepper
flat leaf parsley leaves, to garnish
lemon wedges, to serve

COOK'S TIP
These skewers are great for cooking on a barbecue. Cook for about 8 minutes, turning frequently until cooked through.

1 In a shallow dish, combine the oil, lemon rind and juice, garlic, dried chillies and seasoning. Add the chicken pieces and turn to coat. Cover and place in the refrigerator for at least 4 hours, or overnight.

2 When ready to cook, thread the chicken on to eight oiled skewers and cook under a pre-heated grill (broiler) for 6–8 minutes, turning frequently. Garnish with parsley and serve with lemon wedges.

NUTRITION NOTES

Per portion:	
Energy	301Kcal/1258kJ
Protein	18.7g
Fat	25.2g
saturated fat	5.5g
Carbohydrate	0g
Fibre	0g
Calcium	23.8mg

skewered lamb with coriander yogurt

YOU COULD ALSO MAKE THESE KEBABS using lean beef or pork. For extra colour you can alternate pieces of red, orange or yellow pepper, lemon or onions.

Serves 6

900g/2lb lean boneless lamb
1 large onion, grated
3 bay leaves
5 thyme or rosemary sprigs
grated rind and juice of 1 lemon
2.5ml/½ tsp caster (superfine) sugar
75ml/5 tbsp olive oil
salt and ground black pepper
sprigs of rosemary, to garnish
grilled (broiled) lemon wedges, to serve

For the coriander yogurt

150ml/¼ pint/⅔ cup natural (plain) yogurt
15ml/1 tbsp chopped fresh mint
15ml/1 tbsp chopped fresh
 coriander (cilantro)
10ml/2 tsp grated onion

1 To make the coriander yogurt, put the yogurt, mint, coriander and grated onion in a bowl and mix well to combine. Transfer the coriander yogurt to a small serving dish and chill until ready to serve.

2 To make the kebabs, cut the lamb into small chunks and put in a bowl. In a separate bowl, combine the grated onion, bay leaves, thyme or rosemary sprigs, lemon rind and juice, sugar and olive oil, then add salt and ground black pepper and pour over the lamb.

3 Mix thoroughly to make sure the lamb is well coated. Cover with clear film (plastic wrap) and leave to marinate in the refrigerator for several hours or overnight.

4 Drain the meat and thread on to skewers. Arrange on a grill (broiler) rack and grilll for about 10 minutes until browned, turning occasionally. Transfer to a plate and garnish with rosemary. Serve with grilled lemon wedges and coriander yogurt.

NUTRITION NOTES

Per portion:	
Energy	536Kcal/2240kJ
Protein	47.7g
Fat	35.3g
saturated fat	10.9g
Carbohydrate	6.9g
Fibre	0.8g
Calcium	90.7mg

barbecue-cooked lamb steaks with red pepper salsa

DELICIOUS, JUICY STEAKS are rich in B vitamins, zinc and iron. Lamb steaks cut across the leg make a healthier option as they are relatively lean.

3 Grill (broil) the marinated steaks over a hot barbecue or under a pre-heated gr (broiler), if you prefer. Cook for 2–5 minutes on each side, depending on how well done you want the meat.

4 While the lamb steaks are cooking, quickly prepare the salsa. Place the roasted red peppers, chopped garlic, chives and remaining olive oil in a small bowl and stir well to combine.

5 When the lamb steaks are cooked, serve them immediately with the salsa, either spooned on to the plate or served separately. Garnish the steaks with lettuce and sprigs of flat leaf parsley.

Serves 6

6 lamb steaks
about 15g/½oz fresh rosemary leaves
3 garlic cloves, 2 sliced and
  1 finely chopped
90ml/6 tbsp olive oil
200g/7oz red (bell) peppers, roasted,
  peeled, seeded and chopped
15ml/1 tbsp chopped chives
salt and ground black pepper
lettuce and fresh flat leaf parsley, to garnish

1 Place the lamb steaks in a shallow dish in a single layer and season with salt and ground black pepper. Sprinkle the rosemary leaves and slices of garlic over the meat, then drizzle over with 60ml/ 4 tbsp of the olive oil.

2 Cover the dish with clear film (plastic wrap) and place in the refrigerator to marinate until ready to cook. The steaks can be left to marinate for up to 24 hours.

NUTRITION NOTES

Per portion:	
Energy	275Kcal/1149kJ
Protein	30.5g
Fat	16.2g
saturated fat	6.3g
Carbohydrate	1.7g
Fibre	0.4g
Calcium	20.1mg

stir-fried beef and mushrooms with garlic and black beans

erves 4

0ml/2 tbsp dark soy sauce
0ml/2 tbsp Chinese rice wine
0ml/2 tsp cornflour (cornstarch)
0ml/2 tsp sesame oil
·50g/1lb fillet (beef tenderloin) or rump
  (round) steak, trimmed of fat
2 dried shiitake mushrooms
·5ml/1½ tbsp salted black beans
·ml/1 tsp caster (superfine) sugar
·0ml/4 tbsp groundnut (peanut) oil
· garlic cloves, thinly sliced
2.5cm/1in piece fresh root ginger, cut into
  fine strips
·00g/7oz open cap mushrooms, sliced
· bunch spring onions (scallions),
  sliced diagonally
· fresh red chilli, seeded and shredded
·alt and ground black pepper

In a large bowl, mix together half the
dark soy sauce, half the rice wine, half
he cornflour and all the sesame oil with
·5ml/1 tbsp cold water until smooth and
horoughly combined. Add a generous
·inch of salt and pepper.

2 Cut the beef into very thin slices, no
more than 5mm/¼in thick. Add the
·lices to the cornflour mixture and rub the
·nixture into the beef with your fingers. Set
·aside for 30 minutes.

3 Meanwhile, pour boiling water over
the dried mushrooms and leave to soak
·or 25 minutes. Drain, reserving 45ml/
3 tbsp of the soaking water. Remove and
·discard the stalks and cut the caps in half.

4 Mash the beans with the sugar. In
another bowl, combine the remaining
cornflour, soy sauce and rice wine.

5 Heat the oil in a wok, then stir-fry the
beef for 30–45 seconds, until just
brown. Transfer it to a plate. Pour off some
oil to leave about 45ml/3 tbsp in the wok.

THIS CLASSIC CHINESE DISH is low in fat and offers a good supply of minerals needed for optimum health including zinc and iron. Serve with steamed vegetables such as broccoli.

6 Add the garlic and ginger to the wok,
stir-fry for 1 minute, then add all the
mushrooms and stir-fry for 2 minutes. Set
aside a few tablespoons of the green part
of the spring onions, then add the rest to
the wok. Add the black beans and stir-fry
for 1–2 minutes. Stir in the beef, then add
the shiitake soaking water. Stir in the
cornflour mixture and simmer until the sauce
thickens. Sprinkle the chilli and reserved
spring onions over the beef and serve.

NUTRITION NOTES

Per portion:

Energy	169Kcal/706kJ
Protein	26.1g
Fat	6.8g
saturated fat	2.2g
Carbohydrate	0.9g
Fibre	0.4g
Calcium	30.8mg

low-carb
side dishes

EATING PLENTY OF VEGETABLES and salads is an essential part of any healthy diet. All vegetables contain carbohydrate but some contain more than others, and some are absorbed more gradually, which helps to maintain steady blood sugar levels. Starchy vegetables such as potatoes and yams, which can contain over 35g of rapidly-absorbed carbohydrate per serving, are strictly off limits, and sweet-tasting vegetables such as carrots, which tend to be higher in carbohydrate than most green and leafy vegetables, should be eaten in moderation.

mixed green leaf and herb salad

THIS FLAVOURFUL SALAD makes an ideal side dish that goes well with meat and fish. You could turn it into a more substantial dish for a light lunch by adding one of the variations.

2 To make the dressing, blend together the olive oil and cider vinegar in a small bowl and season with salt and ground black pepper to taste.

3 Place the mixed herbs and salad leaves in a large salad bowl. Just before serving, pour over the dressing and toss thoroughly to mix well, using your hands. Serve immediately.

VARIATIONS

To make a more substantial salad for a light lunch or supper, try adding some of the following ingredients:
• Baby broad (fava) beans, sliced artichoke hearts and quartered hard-boiled eggs
• Cooked chickpeas, asparagus tips and pitted green olives.

Serves 4

15g/½oz/½ cup mixed fresh herbs, such as chervil, tarragon (use sparingly), dill, basil, marjoram (use sparingly), flat leaf parsley, mint, sorrel, fennel and coriander (cilantro)

350g/12oz mixed salad leaves, such as rocket (arugula), radicchio, chicory (Belgian endive), watercress, frisée, baby spinach, oakleaf lettuce and dandelion

For the dressing

50ml/2fl oz/¼ cup extra virgin olive oil
15ml/1 tbsp cider vinegar
salt and ground black pepper

1 Wash and dry the herbs and salad leaves in a salad spinner, or use two clean, dry dishtowels to pat them dry.

NUTRITION NOTES

Per portion:	
Energy	111Kcal/463kJ
Protein	0.7g
Fat	11.4g
saturated fat	1.7g
Carbohydrate	1.5g
Fibre	0.8g
Calcium	24.5mg

spinach and roast garlic salad

SIMPLE LEAFY SALADS are the perfect accompaniment to any main meal. Spinach offers a good supply of vitamin C, folates and potassium, and garlic is reputed to have health-giving properties and is a natural anti-viral and anti-bacterial agent.

rves 4
2 garlic cloves, unpeeled
0ml/4 tbsp extra virgin olive oil
0g/1lb baby spinach leaves
)g/2oz/½ cup pine nuts, lightly toasted
ce of ½ lemon
t and ground black pepper

Preheat the oven to 190°C/375°F/ Gas 5. Place the unpeeled garlic cloves in small roasting pan, drizzle over 30ml/ tbsp of the olive oil and toss to coat. Bake about 15 minutes until slightly charred.

Tip the garlic cloves, still in their skins, into a salad bowl. Add the spinach, ne nuts, lemon juice and remaining olive . Toss well and season with salt and epper. Serve immediately, squeezing the ftened garlic purée out of the skins to eat.

NUTRITION NOTES

Per portion:

Energy	222Kcal/927kJ
Protein	5.7g
Fat	20.5g
saturated fat	2.36g
Carbohydrate	3.9g
Fibre	3g
Calcium	194mg

COOK'S TIPS
• When spinach is served raw in a salad, the leaves need to be young and tender. Wash them well, drain and pat them dry with kitchen paper.
• Don't worry about the large amount of garlic used in this salad. Roasting subdues garlic's pungent flavour and it will become sweet and subtle, while retaining its health-giving properties.

asparagus with lemon sauce

THIS SOPHISTICATED DISH is higher in carbohydrate than a simple green salad but it makes a wonderful vegetable accompaniment for a special dinner.

Serves 4
675g/1½lb asparagus, tough
   ends removed, and tied in
   a bundle
15ml/1 tbsp cornflour (cornstarch)
2 egg yolks
juice of 1½ lemons
salt

1 Cook the asparagus in a pan of salted boiling water for 8 minutes. Drain well and arrange in a serving dish. Reserve 200ml/ 7fl oz/scant 1 cup of the cooking liquid.

2 In a small bowl, blend the cornflour with the cooled, reserved cooking liquid, then pour into a small pan. Bring the mixture to the boil, stirring, and cook over a gentle heat until the sauce thickens slightly. Remove the pan from the heat and set aside to cool for a few minutes.

3 In a bowl, beat the egg yolks with the lemon juice, then gradually stir the mixture into the cooled sauce. Cook over a very low heat, stirring constantly, until the sauce is fairly thick. Do not overheat.

4 As soon as the sauce has thickened, remove the pan from the heat and continue stirring for 1 minute. Taste and add a little salt if necessary. Allow the sauce to cool slightly.

5 Once cooled, stir the sauce, then pour a little over the asparagus. Cover the dish with clear film (plastic wrap) and chill for at least 2 hours before serving with the rest of the sauce handed separately.

VARIATIONS
This sauce goes very well with all sorts of young vegetables, such as baby leeks and green beans.

NUTRITION NOTES

Per portion:

Energy	126Kcal/526k
Protein	6.5g
Fat	3.8g
saturated fat	0.9g
Carbohydrate	7.3g
Fibre	2.9g
Calcium	60mg

Florets polonaise

STEAMED VEGETABLES are a delicious and extremely healthy accompaniment for any main meal. If you want to reduce the carbohydrate content further, omit the breadcrumbs.

Serves 6

500g/1¼lb cauliflower and broccoli
finely grated rind of ½ lemon
1 large garlic clove, crushed
25g/1oz/½ cup wholegrain
  breadcrumbs, lightly baked or
  grilled (broiled) until crisp
2 eggs, hard-boiled and shelled
salt and ground black pepper

NUTRITION NOTES

Per portion:

Energy	73Kcal/305kJ
Protein	5.7g
Fat	2.7g
saturated fat	0.7g
Carbohydrate	7.1g
Fibre	1.5g
Calcium	33.4mg

1 Trim the cauliflower and broccoli, break into florets and place in a steamer over a pan of boiling water and steam for about 12 minutes. If you prefer, boil the vegetables in salted water for 5–7 minutes, until just tender. Drain the vegetables well and transfer to a warmed serving dish.

2 While the vegetables are cooking, make the topping. In a bowl, combine the lemon rind, garlic and breadcrumbs. Finely chop the eggs and mix into the breadcrumb mixture. Season with salt and black pepper to taste, then sprinkle the chopped egg mixture over the cooked vegetables and serve.

VARIATIONS
Sprinkle the egg topping over other steamed vegetables such as courgettes (zucchini) or spring greens (collards).

broccoli with garlic

THIS LOW-FAT, LOW-CARBOHYDRATE vegetable is high in vitamins and minerals, notably iron and folates. Amazingly, it is an even better source of vitamin C than oranges.

1 Using a sharp knife, trim off and discard the thick stems from the broccoli, and cut the head into large, even-size florets.

2 Bring a large pan of water to the boil. Add the broccoli florets and cook for about 3 minutes, until just tender but still retaining its bite.

3 Drain the broccoli well and arrange the florets in a warmed serving dish.

NUTRITION NOTES

Per portion:

Energy	61Kcal/254kJ
Protein	4.9g
Fat	3.7g
saturated fat	0.5g
Carbohydrate	2.0g
Fibre	2.9g
Calcium	63mg

Serves 4

450g/1lb broccoli
15ml/1 tbsp sunflower oil
2 garlic cloves, crushed
fried garlic slices, to garnish (optional)

VARIATION

Use any other steamed or boiled green vegetable such as pak choi (bok choy) or spinach in place of the broccoli.

4 Heat the sunflower oil in a small pan, add the crushed garlic and cook for about 2 minutes, being careful not to let it burn, then remove the garlic with a slotted spoon and discard.

5 Pour the garlic-flavoured oil over the broccoli. Sprinkle with fried garlic slices, if using, and serve immediately.

ried spring greens

GREEN LEAFY VEGETABLES make an excellent choice for a low-carbohydrate accompaniment. They are rich in essential nutrients and full of valuable fibre.

rves 4
5ml/1 tbsp olive oil
5g/3oz rindless smoked streaky (fatty)
bacon, chopped
large onion, thinly sliced
garlic cloves, finely chopped
)0g/2lb spring greens
(collards), shredded
lt and ground black pepper

VARIATION
Use shredded red cabbage in place of the spring greens. Leave to simmer for 10 minutes longer as red cabbage is tougher and requires longer cooking.

1 In a large frying pan, heat the oil and add the bacon. Fry for 2 minutes, then add the onion and garlic and fry for 3 minutes more until the onion begins to soften.

2 Reduce the heat and add the spring greens and season. Cook, covered, over a gentle heat for about 15 minutes until the greens are tender. Serve immediately.

NUTRITION NOTES

Per portion:	
Energy	197Kcal/823kJ
Protein	10.4g
Fat	12.3g
saturated fat	2.5g
Carbohydrate	11.7g
Fibre	8.5g
Calcium	488mg

roasted plum tomatoes and garlic

DESPITE THE SWEET FLAVOUR of roasted tomatoes, this dish is actually very low in carbohydrate and makes a healthy and nutritious accompaniment to grilled fish, poultry or meat.

Serves 4

8 plum tomatoes, halved
12 garlic cloves
60ml/4 tbsp extra virgin olive oil
3 bay leaves
salt and ground black pepper
fresh oregano leaves, to garnish

NUTRITION NOTES

Per portion:

Energy	125Kcal/522kJ
Protein	1.4g
Fat	11.3g
saturated fat	1.6g
Carbohydrate	4.6g
Fibre	1.4g
Calcium	8.8mg

1 Preheat the oven to 230°C/450°F/ Gas 8. Select an ovenproof dish that will hold all the tomatoes snugly in a single layer.

2 Arrange the halved tomatoes in the dish and push the whole, unpeeled garlic cloves between them.

3 Brush the tomatoes with the oil, add the bay leaves and sprinkle with pepper. Bake for 45 minutes until the tomatoes have softened and are sizzling in the dish. They should be charred around the edges. Season with salt and a little more black pepper, if needed. Garnish with oregano and serve.

okra with coriander and tomatoes

THIS AROMATIC DISH is delicious hot or cold and makes a good accompaniment at any time of the year. It is rich in valuable nutrients including vitamins C and E and potassium.

Serves 4

450g/1lb tomatoes or 400g/
  14oz can chopped tomatoes
450g/1lb fresh okra
45ml/3 tbsp olive oil
2 onions, thinly sliced
10ml/2 tsp coriander seeds, crushed
3 garlic cloves, crushed
finely grated rind and juice
  of 1 lemon
salt and ground black pepper

1 If using fresh tomatoes, cut a cross in the stalk ends, plunge them into boiling water for about 30 seconds, then refresh in cold water. Peel off the skins and chop the flesh, discarding the tough core.

2 Trim off any stalks from the okra and discard, leaving the okra whole. Heat the olive oil in a frying pan and cook the onions and coriander seeds for 3–4 minutes, or until just beginning to colour.

3 Add the okra and garlic to the pan and cook for 1 minute. Stir in the tomatoes and simmer gently for 20 minutes until the okra is tender. Stir in the lemon rind and juice and add seasoning. Serve warm or cold.

NUTRITION NOTES

Per portion:	
Energy	73Kcal/305kJ
Protein	5.7g
Fat	2.7g
saturated fat	0.7g
Carbohydrate	7.1g
Fibre	1.5g
Calcium	33.4mg

leek terrine with red peppers

THIS CHILLED VEGETABLE dish is a good source of fibre
and provides many of the nutrients essential for good health,
including vitamin C, betacarotene and bioflavenoids.

4 Layer the leeks and strips of red pepper
in the lined tin, alternating the layers
and finishing with a layer of roasted pepper.
Season the leeks with a little more salt and
ground black pepper.

5 Cover the terrine with the overhanging
clear film. Top with a plate and weigh
down with heavy food cans or scale weights.
Chill for several hours or overnight.

6 To make the dressing, place the oil,
garlic, mustard, soy sauce and vinegar in
a jug (pitcher) and mix thoroughly. Season to
taste with salt and pepper. Add ground cumin
to taste and leave to stand for several hours.
Discard the garlic and stir in the fresh herbs.

7 When ready to serve, carefully unmould
the terrine and cut it into thick slices.
Serve drizzled with the dressing.

Serves 6

1.8kg/4lb slender leeks
4 large red (bell) peppers, halved
    and seeded
15ml/1 tbsp extra virgin olive oil
10ml/2 tsp balsamic vinegar
5ml/1 tsp ground roasted cumin seeds
salt and ground black pepper

For the dressing

60ml/4 tbsp extra virgin olive oil
1 garlic clove, bruised and peeled
5ml/1 tsp Dijon mustard
5ml/1 tsp soy sauce
15ml/1 tbsp balsamic vinegar
2.5–5ml/½–1 tsp ground roasted
    cumin seeds
15–30ml/1–2 tbsp chopped mixed fresh
    basil and flat leaf parsley

1 Line a 23cm/9in-long terrine or loaf tin
(pan) with clear film (plastic wrap), leaving
the ends overhanging the tin. Carefully cut the
leeks to the same length as the tin.

2 Cook the leeks in salted boiling water for
5–7 minutes, or until just tender. Drain
thoroughly and leave to cool, then squeeze
out as much water as possible from the leeks
and leave them to drain on a clean dishtowel.

3 Grill (broil) the red peppers, skin-side
uppermost, until the skin blisters and
blackens. Place in a bowl, cover and leave
for 10 minutes. Peel the peppers and cut the
flesh into long strips, then place them in a
bowl and pour over the oil and balsamic
vinegar and sprinkle with the cumin. Season
to taste with salt and pepper and toss well.

NUTRITION NOTES

Per portion:	
Energy	149Kcal/622kJ
Protein	5.8g
Fat	7.4g
saturated fat	1.2g
Carbohydrate	15.5g
Fibre	8.3g
Calcium	80.5mg

adicchio and chicory gratin

BAKING SALAD VEGETABLES in a creamy sauce creates a dish that is wholesome, warming and sustaining. It will fill you up, but won't load on the carbohydrate.

erves 4

heads radicchio, quartered lengthways
heads chicory (Belgian endive),
  quartered lengthways
5g/1oz/½ cup drained sun-dried
  tomatoes in oil, coarsely chopped
5g/1oz/2 tbsp butter
5g/½oz/2 tbsp plain (all-purpose) flour
50ml/8fl oz/1 cup milk
inch of freshly grated nutmeg
0g/2oz/½ cup grated Emmenthal cheese
alt and ground black pepper

Preheat the oven to 180°C/350°F/
Gas 4. Grease a 1.2 litre/2 pint/5 cup
venproof dish and arrange the radicchio
nd chicory in it. Sprinkle over the sun-dried
omatoes and brush the vegetables with oil
om the jar. Season and cover the dish
vith foil. Bake for 15 minutes, then uncover
nd bake for a further 10 minutes.

NUTRITION NOTES

Per portion:

Energy	173Kcal/723kJ
Protein	6.6g
Fat	13.4g
saturated fat	6.9g
Carbohydrate	8.1g
Fibre	0.7g
Calcium	217mg

2 To make the sauce, place the butter in a small pan and melt over a medium heat. When the butter is foaming, add the flour and cook for 1 minute, stirring. Remove from the heat and gradually add the milk, whisking all the time. Return to the heat and bring to the boil, then simmer for about 3 minutes to thicken. Season to taste and add the nutmeg.

3 Pour the sauce over the vegetables and sprinkle with the cheese. Bake for about 20 minutes until golden. Serve immediately.

VARIATION
Use fennel in place of the radicchio and chicory. Par-boil the fennel first.

desserts

FOR THOSE WITH A SWEET TOOTH, sticking to a low-carbohydrate diet and avoiding all things sweet and indulgent may sound like the impossible. However, there are plenty of sweet treats that won't ruin your diet if eaten occasionally. This chapter brings together a selection of delicious desserts that are relatively low in carbohydrate and will make the perfect end to a special meal.

fresh fruit salad

A LIGHT AND REFRESHING fruit salad makes a healthy and nutritious end to a low-carbohydrate meal. The natural fruit sugars are kinder to the body than refined sugars.

Serves 6
2 peaches
2 oranges
2 eating apples
16–20 strawberries
30ml/2 tbsp lemon juice
15–30ml/1–2 tbsp orange flower water
a few fresh mint leaves, to decorate

Per portion:

Energy	39Kcal/163kJ
Protein	0.8g
Fat	0.1g
saturated fat	0.0g
Carbohydrate	9.3g
Fibre	1.6g
Calcium	9.9mg

1 Place the peaches in a bowl and pour over boiling water. Leave to stand for 1 minute, then lift out with a slotted spoon, peel, stone and cut the flesh into thick slices.

2 Peel the oranges with a sharp knife, removing all the white pith, and segment them, catching any juice in a bowl.

3 Peel and core the apples and cut into thin slices. Using the point of a knife, hull the strawberries and halve or quarter the fruits if they are large. Place all the prepared fruit in a large serving bowl.

4 Blend together the lemon juice, orange flower water and any reserved orange juice. Pour the fruit juice mixture over the salad and toss lightly. Serve decorated with a few fresh mint leaves.

fruit platter with spices

A SIMPLE FRESH fruit platter sprinkled with spices makes a healthy dessert. It is low in fat and offers a range of essential vitamins and minerals that are needed for good health.

Serves 6

1 pineapple
2 papayas
1 small melon
juice of 2 limes
2 pomegranates
ground ginger and ground nutmeg,
    for sprinkling
mint sprigs, to decorate

1 Peel the pineapple. Remove the core and any remaining eyes, then cut the flesh lengthways into thin wedges. Peel the papayas, cut them in half, and then into thin wedges. Halve the melon and remove the seeds. Cut into thin wedges and remove the skin. Arrange the fruit on six individual plates and sprinkle with the lime juice.

2 Cut the pomegranates in half using a sharp knife, then scoop out the seeds, discarding any pith. Sprinkle the seeds over the fruit, then sprinkle the salad with a little ginger and nutmeg to taste. Decorate with sprigs of fresh mint and serve immediately.

VARIATION

The selection of fruit can be varied according to what is available. Guava and mango make an exotic combination but oranges and plums are also good.

NUTRITION NOTES

Per portion:

Energy	55Kcal/229kJ
Protein	1g
Fat	0.3g
saturated fat	0g
Carbohydrate	12.9g
Fibre	2.3g
Calcium	25.3mg

pistachio kulfi ice cream

THIS CLASSIC INDIAN DESSERT, made from milk and nuts, contains more carbohydrate than some other desserts, but it can still be enjoyed as an occasional treat. The milk and nuts provide a good source of protein.

3 Strain the reduced milk into a bowl or jug (pitcher), and discard the cardamom pods and seeds. Stir the sugar into the milk and set the mixture aside to cool.

4 Meanwhile, place half the nuts in a blender and grind to a smooth powder. Cut the remaining nuts into thin slivers and set them aside for decoration.

5 Stir the ground nuts into the cooled milk mixture. Pour into four kulfi moulds and freeze overnight until firm.

6 To unmould the kulfi, half fill a bowl with very hot water. Stand each mould in the water and count to ten. Immediately lift it out and invert the ice cream on to individual serving plates. Decorate with sliced pistachio nuts and rose petals and serve immediately.

NUTRITION NOTES

Per portion:	
Energy	272Kcal/1135kJ
Protein	14.61g
Fat	12.93g
saturated fat	4.63g
Carbohydrate	26.34g
Fibre	0.76g
Calcium	464.38mg

Serves 4

1.5 litres/2½ pints/6¼ cups semi-skimmed (low-fat) milk
3 cardamom pods
25g/1oz/2 tbsp caster (superfine) sugar
50g/2oz/½ cup pistachio nuts, skinned plus a few to decorate
a few pink rose petals, to decorate

1 Pour the milk into a large heavy pan and bring to the boil. Lower the heat and simmer for one hour, stirring occasionally.

2 Crush the cardamom pods in a mortar with a pestle, then add them to the milk. Simmer the mixture for 1½ hours, or until the milk has reduced to 475ml/16fl oz/2 cups.

rhubarb and ginger yogurt ice

FROZEN YOGURT flavoured with fruit makes a healthy alternative to ice cream. It is low in fat and high in calcium, which is essential for good bone health.

Serves 6

300g/11oz/scant 1½ cups set natural (plain) live yogurt
200g/7oz/scant 1 cup mascarpone
350g/12oz/3 cups chopped rhubarb
30ml/2 tbsp clear honey
3 pieces preserved stem ginger, finely chopped

1 In a bowl, whisk together the yogurt and mascarpone. Pour the yogurt mixture into a shallow freezerproof container and freeze for about 1 hour.

2 Meanwhile, put the chopped rhubarb and honey in a large pan and add 45ml/3 tbsp water. Cook over a very low heat, stirring occasionally, for 15 minutes, or until the rhubarb is soft. Remove the pan from the heat and set aside to cool. When the fruit has cooled, place it in a food processor or blender and process to a purée.

3 Remove the semi-frozen yogurt mixture from the freezer and fold in the rhubarb purée. Beat well until smooth, breaking up the ice crystals, then fold in the chopped ginger.

4 Return the yogurt ice to the freezer and freeze for 2 hours. Remove from the freezer and beat again, then freeze until solid. To serve, scoop the yogurt ice into individual serving bowls.

NUTRITION NOTES

Per portion:	
Energy	84Kcal/350kJ
Protein	5.0g
Fat	3.9g
saturated fat	2.5g
Carbohydrate	7.7g
Fibre	0.2g
Calcium	159mg

COOK'S TIPS

• To make serving easier, take the yogurt ice out of the freezer and transfer it to the refrigerator about 15 minutes before serving to allow it to soften sufficiently to scoop easily.
• Make sure that you remove all traces of the leaves from rhubarb as they contain the poison oxalic acid.

peach and cardamom yogurt ice

LOW-FAT FROZEN DESSERTS that rely on natural fruit for their sweetness make the perfect low-carbohydrate dessert. This yogurt ice provides a useful source of calcium and vitamin C.

2 Chop the peaches and put them in a pan. Add the crushed cardamom pods, with their black seeds, and the measured water. Cover and simmer gently for about 10 minutes, or until the fruit is tender. Remove the pan from the heat and leave to cool.

3 Tip the peach mixture into a food processor or blender, process until smooth, then press through a sieve placed over a bowl.

4 Add the yogurt to the sieved purée and mix together in the bowl. Pour into a plastic freezerproof tub and freeze for about 6 hours until firm, beating once or twice with a fork, electric whisk or in a food processor to break up the ice crystals.

5 To serve, scoop the ice cream on to a large platter or into individual bowls.

Serves 4
8 cardamom pods
6 peaches, total weight about 500g/1¼lb, halved and stoned (pitted)
30ml/2 tbsp water
200ml/7fl oz/scant 1 cup bio natural (plain) yogurt

COOK'S TIP
Use bio natural (plain) yogurt for its extra mild taste. Greek (US strained plain) yogurt or ordinary natural yogurt are both much sharper, and tend to overwhelm the delicate taste of peach.

1 Put the cardamom pods on a board and crush them with the base of a ramekin, or use a mortar and pestle.

NUTRITION NOTES

Per portion:	
Energy	126Kcal/596kJ
Protein	8.22g
Fat	6.9g
saturated fat	4.3g
Carbohydrate	8g
Fibre	1.2g
Calcium	168mg

fruit-filled soufflé omelette

A LIGHT AND FLUFFY soufflé omelette filled with fresh, juicy strawberries is a decadent and indulgent treat that's naturally low in carbohydrate.

Serves 3

75g/3oz/¾ cup strawberries, hulled
3 eggs, separated
30ml/2 tbsp caster (superfine) sugar
45ml/3 tbsp double (heavy)
  cream, whipped
a few drops of vanilla essence (extract)
25g/1oz/2 tbsp butter

Hull the strawberries and cut them in half. Set aside. In a bowl, beat the egg yolks and sugar until pale and fluffy, then fold in the cream and vanilla essence. Whisk the egg whites in a very large, grease-free bowl until stiff, then carefully fold into the yolks.

2 Melt the butter in an omelette pan. When sizzling, pour in the egg mixture and cook until set underneath, shaking occasionally. Spoon on the strawberries and, tilting the pan, slide the omelette so that it folds over.

3 Carefully slide the omelette on to a warm serving plate. Cut the omelette into three pieces, then transfer to three warmed plates and serve immediately.

VARIATION
Use any type of soft, non-starchy fruit in place of the strawberries. Slices of peach, fresh berries or a combination of several fruits will all work well.

NUTRITION NOTES

Per portion:	
Energy	205Kcal/854kJ
Protein	7.57g
Fat	14.2g
saturated fat	6.78g
Carbohydrate	12.48g
Fibre	0.29g
Calcium	51mg

baked ricotta cakes with red sauce

THESE HONEY- AND VANILLA-FLAVOURED cakes are a tasty
treat for a special meal. Try not to add too much extra honey to
the sauce because it will add to the total carbohydrate content.

Serves 4

250g/9oz/generous 1 cup ricotta cheese
2 egg whites, beaten
30ml/2 tbsp clear honey, plus extra
   to taste
5ml/1 tsp vanilla essence (extract)
450g/1lb/4 cups mixed fresh or
   frozen fruit, such as strawberries,
   raspberries, blackberries
   and cherries
fresh mint leaves, to decorate (optional)

1 Preheat the oven to 180°C/350°F/
Gas 4. Place the ricotta cheese in a bowl
and break it up with a wooden spoon. Add
the beaten egg whites, honey and vanilla
essence and mix thoroughly until the mixture is
smooth and well combined.

2 Lightly grease four ramekins. Spoon the
ricotta mixture into the ramekins and
level the tops. Bake for 20 minutes, or until
the ricotta cakes are risen and golden.

3 Meanwhile, make the fruit sauce.
Reserve about a quarter of the fruit for
decoration. Place the rest of the fruit in a
pan, with a little water if the fruit is fresh, and
heat gently until softened. Remove the pan
from the heat and leave to cool slightly.
Remove any cherry pits, if using cherries.

4 Press the fruit through a sieve, then taste
and sweeten with honey if it is too tart.
Serve the sauce, warm or cold, with the
ricotta cakes. Decorate with the reserved
berries and mint leaves, if using.

COOK'S TIP

If using frozen fruit for the sauce, there
is no need to add extra water because
there are usually plenty of ice crystals
clinging to the berries. Adding extra
water may make the sauce too runny.

NUTRITION NOTES

Per portion:

Energy	366Kcal/1525kJ
Protein	25.9g
Fat	24.8g
saturated fat	12.4g
Carbohydrate	11.3g
Fibre	3.7g
Calcium	747mg

checking carbohydrate content

THE FOLLOWING LIST shows the glycaemic index (GI) and carbohydrate (CARB) content of many common foods. When choosing foods, aim for those with a low GI, which indicates that they are absorbed slowly into the bloodstream, and a low carbohydrate content.

FOOD	PORTION	GI	CARB
apple	1 fruit	38	18g
apple juice	250ml	40	33g
apricots	3 fruits	57	7g
bagel, white	1	72	35g
baked beans	120g	48	13g
banana	1 fruit	55	32g
barley	80g	25	17g
beetroot (beet)	60g	64	5g
biscuits (cookies)			
Digestives	2 biscuits	59	21g
morning coffee	3 biscuits	79	14g
shortbread	2 biscuits	64	19g
black beans	120g	43	16g
black-eyed beans (peas)	120g	42	24g
breads			
baguette	30g	95	15g
fruit loaf	1 slice	47	18g
pitta bread	1 piece	57	38g
pumpernickel	1 slice	41	35g
rye bread	1 slice	65	23g
white	1 slice	70	15g
wholemeal (whole-wheat)	1 slice	69	14g
breakfast cereals			
All-Bran	40g	42	22g
Cheerios	30g	74	20g
Cornflakes	30g	84	26g
muesli	60g	56	32g
porridge (oatmeal)	245g	42	24g
puffed wheat	30g	80	22g
Rice Krispies	30g	82	27g
broad beans	80g	79	9g
buckwheat	80g	54	57g
bulgur wheat	120g	48	22g
butter beans	70g	31	13g
cakes			
banana cake	1 slice	47	46g
sponge cake	1 slice	46	32g
cantaloupe	¼ small fruit	65	10g

FOOD	PORTION	GI	CARB
carrots	70g	49	3g
cherries	20 fruits	22	10g
chickpeas	120g	33	22g
chocolate, milk	30g	49	19g
corn chips	50g	42	33g
cornmeal	40g	68	30g
couscous	120g	65	28g
croissant	1	67	27g
crumpet	1	69	22g
custard	175g	43	24g
doughnut	40g	76	16g
fish fingers	5 fingers	38	24g
gnocchi	145g	68	71g
grapefruit	½ fruit	25	5g
grapefruit juice	250ml	48	16g
grapes	100g	46	15g
haricot (navy) beans	90g	38	11g
honey	15ml	58	16g
ice cream	2 scoops	61	10g
kidney beans	90g	27	18g
kiwi fruit	1 fruit	52	8g
lentils	95g	30	16g
lychees, canned	7 fruits	79	16g
mango	1 small fruit	55	19g
milk, full fat	250ml	27	12g
milk, skimmed	250ml	32	13g
muffin, apple	80g	10	44g
noodles	85g	46	55g
nuts (see peanuts)			
orange	1 fruit	44	10g
orange juice	250ml	46	21g
papaya	½ fruit	58	14g
parsnips	75g	97	8g
pasta			
spaghetti, white	180g	41	56g
spaghetti wholemeal (whole-wheat)	180g	41	56g
tortellini	180g	50	21g
pastry	65g	59	25g
peach	1 fruit	42	7g

FOOD	PORTION	GI	CARB
peanuts	75g	14	11g
pear	1 fruit	38	21g
peas	80g	48	5g
pineapple	2 slices	66	10g
pizza	2 slices	60	57g
plums	3 fruits	39	7g
popcorn	20g	55	10g
potatoes			
baked	120g	85	14g
boiled	120g	56	16g
crisps (US chips)	50g	54	24g
French fries	120g	75	49g
mashed	120g	70	16g
pretzels	50g	83	22g
pumpkin	85g	75	6g
raisins	40g	64	28g
rice			
white basmati	180g	58	50g
white glutinous	175g	98	37g
rice cakes	2	82	21g
soya beans	100g	14	12g
sweetcorn	85g	54	16g
sweet potato	80g	54	16g
watermelon	150g	72	8g
yogurt, fruit	200g	33	26g

index